Building a Learning Culture in America

Building a Learning Culture in America

Kevin P. Chavous

Transaction Publishers
New Brunswick (U.S.A.) and London (U.K.)

Library of Congress Catalog Number: 2016024569
ISBN: 978-1-4128-6418-3 (hardcover); 978-1-4128-6442-8 (paper)
eBook: 978-1-4128-6381-0
Printed in the United States of America

Library of Congress Cataloging-in-Publication Data

Names: Chavous, Kevin P., author.
Title: Building a learning culture in America / Kevin P. Chavous.
Description: New Brunswick, New Jersey : Transaction Publishers, [2016] | Includes bibliographical references and index.
Identifiers: LCCN 2016024569 (print) | LCCN 2016033354 (ebook) | ISBN 9781412864183 (hardcover) | ISBN 9781412864428 (pbk.) | ISBN 9781412863810
Subjects: LCSH: Education--United States. | Public schools--United States. | Education--Aims and objectives--United States. | Education--Social aspects--United States.
Classification: LCC LA217.2 .C497 2016 (print) | LCC LA217.2 (ebook) | DDC 370.973--dc23
LC record available at https://lccn.loc.gov/2016024569

This book is dedicated to those American children yet unborn, precious in God's light, all certain to be born full of the joy and wonder of life. May the bright light of curiosity that they possess when they come to this world continue to shine, be nurtured, and grow continuously throughout their lives.

Contents

Part 3. Some Success Stories

Foreword

It gives me immense pleasure and a great deal of pride to have the opportunity to write the Foreword for this extraordinary book. *Building a Learning Culture in America* is authored by a remarkable man and cherished friend. Kevin P. Chavous, lawyer, politician, humanitarian, civil rights activist, prayerful Christian, star college basketball player, and an unrelenting education reformer, is, in my view, an under-celebrated American hero. And for those who think I am laying it on a little too thick, check back with me after you have finished reading this book.

I met Kevin shortly after I arrived in Washington, DC, as the nation's seventh US secretary of education. One day I was scheduled to make remarks at a program sponsored by the District of Columbia public schools. It took place at one of the district's high schools. As I, along with others on the program, gathered on the dais, a tall, well-dressed gentleman came up to me and introduced himself as Kevin Chavous. In my role as secretary of education I was constantly inundated with people introducing themselves to me, so this was nothing special. But when Kevin took the mic and began to speak, I, along with the rest of the audience, was captivated by his presentation. The clarity of his message, the passion of his delivery, and the sincerity of his expression were mesmerizing. It was clear to me that he was not just another political climber; he was someone special.

My initial assessment of Kevin was right, as other interactions with him authenticated, and this impressive book, *Building a Learning Culture in America*, makes it clear. Through the years, Kevin's accomplishments have continued to demonstrate his distinctness. Without him, there would be no DC Opportunity Scholarship Program. Without him, there would be no Democrats for Education

Reform (DFER). Without him, there would be much less energy in the school reform and parental choice movements.

Kevin begins *Building a Learning Culture in America* with a brief overview of his personal history, which gives us a better understanding of the source of his commitment and the character of his personality. He then takes the readers through his long, tenuous, and sometimes painful journey: his membership on the DC City Council, his chairmanship of the City Council's Education Committee, his DC Charter School leadership and advocacy, his prominent role in establishing the DC Opportunity Scholarship Program, losing City Council reelection, and his campaign to become mayor of the District of Columbia. His explanation of the role he played in leading the establishment of the DC Opportunity Scholarship Program was, for me, a powerful and emotional read.

Building a Learning Culture in America is not just another of the massive number of education reform books hitting the market these days. It charts a new path, one based on culture, a little noticed component of the forces influencing educational performance of America's youth. But, as Kevin points out in the book, it may be the most powerful of all the elements determining educational achievement of American youth.

As an experienced education warrior, Kevin recognizes that education is greater than politics—when we allow politics to guide our education policy, we are not acting in a way that benefits our nation's schoolchildren, particularly those who are most at risk. We must use politics to achieve our education goals, not the other way around, something that Kevin has always recognized and which he highlights in *Building a Learning Culture in America*. In the book, Kevin discusses some schools that are doing well by their students: they're surpassing local politics to do what is needed for their kids, and they're improving the quality of education at their schools in leaps and bounds. I visited some of these schools with Kevin and can say without question that this is what we need—more school districts, superintendents, principals, and teachers to be focused on what works for their students. As Kevin would say, it's time to instill a culture of learning in all individuals, students, parents, and administrators alike.

In the Introduction to Part Two of the book Kevin uses the term "Revelation." I believe the sentence "I fervently believe that the next frontier for education is not education itself, but learning as a lifelong avocation" plainly describes Kevin's revelation and also the main idea of the book. This is a bold approach to a long-held intractable issue, but it's patently Kevin Chavous.

As you read the book, my bet is that you will feel pulled into the struggle to improve educational opportunities for America's children, especially the most in need. More importantly, I am confident that you will not only embrace Kevin's vision of a new learning culture in America, but also believe that we have the capacity to create that culture for all of our children. Enjoy!

Dr. Rod Paige
Former Superintendent of the
Houston Independent School District
United States Secretary of Education,
January 2001–January 2005

Preface

This is my education manifesto. It is borne out of nearly twenty years of fighting to improve our schools and expand on the educational opportunities available to our most challenged children. During those twenty years, I have seen firsthand the decay of our schools. And I have also witnessed how we have responded to that decay. Often grounded in good intentions, various reforms have been attempted as a way to right our education system. Though noble in scope, none of those reform initiatives have led to the wholesale change required to make education work for all children.

More than anything, I have become uniquely conversant as to what works and what doesn't. But I am not alone. The sad irony is that most people associated with education know what works. Schools need high standards, high expectations, quality teachers, a great school leader, a willingness to embrace innovation and creativity, and a belief that all children can learn. But if so many of us know what works, why can't we educate our children? Why is it that the light that shines so brightly in the eyes of all kindergartners grows dim for many of those same children by the time they reach fourth grade? While many factors contribute to the answer to that question, such as children's upbringing, the persistent problem with education in America is much more fundamental. The core of our problem lies with us—our values, our priorities, our culture, or rather, the lack thereof. At one time, we were the envy of the world because of the way we embraced education. Consistent with that can-do American spirit, our core belief was that through education and hard work, one could improve one's lot in life. America was nourished by that belief, and our country benefited from it. It was universally believed that each American's "pull yourself up by your bootstraps" story made our country stronger. But over the last forty years or so, we began to lose our way. Increasingly, success wasn't measured by hard work or even education. And today, many view education as a means to an end rather than an essential part of the learning journey of life.

Over the past forty years, the students and teachers who make up our classrooms have changed, while our education bureaucracy has not. Children from diverse backgrounds and with different needs weren't getting what they needed to learn in our traditional schools. Teachers who were tasked with educating these children weren't getting the professional development or support they needed to do their jobs. Slowly but surely, the dumbing down of our schools began. Most of our school districts embraced mediocrity rather than innovation as they struggled with the changing dynamics of the 1960s and 1970s. Soon, the individual learning needs of students took a backseat to the needs of the system. And we became numb to stories like those of children graduating from high school who can't read and statistics about dropout rates and growing achievement gaps.

What's worse, we began to get mired in peripheral fights. Sure, countless reform proposals have been offered in nearly every school district. But as soon as anyone articulates a new education idea or position, that person is placed in a proverbial box, labeled and immediately ostracized by those who think differently and who make up the status quo. It doesn't matter if the idea or proposal will actually help our children; the lines are already drawn in the sand. Sadly, the unknowing public finds itself in the position of having to choose sides, even while they themselves try to understand or navigate our education system for their own children. Politics, patronage, and adult priorities take precedence over the individual education needs of our children, a notion that is unheard of among the vast majority of nations around the world.

Other countries have come to understand that real learning is more important than educational systems and politics. These countries place a premium on the educational opportunities of each child. Over time, many of these countries have developed a culture that celebrates learning and makes learning the focal point of family and community pride.

Here in America, we need to do the same thing. We need an education revolution in our country. One that is designed to truly put the learning interests of children first. A revolution that makes it clear that most of the education issues being discussed are, at best, ancillary to ensuring that there are high-quality learning opportunities available for each and every American child.

But we need to change our culture before a true revolution can emerge.

In this book, my education manifesto, I will focus on that culture change. I will talk about where we have been, where we are, and, more importantly, where we need to be. As you read these pages, you will see how my own personal experiences have helped to shape my views and guide my thinking around how we can fix what's wrong with America's approach to educating its young. Although I did not know it at the time, I was born into a house that contained its own learning culture. Both of my parents, particularly my father, planted learning seeds in my siblings and me such that the quest for knowledge was second nature for all of us. It wasn't until I got to law school that I realized the culture of learning created by my parents in our home was not commonly found in other American households. In their own unique way, my parents kept us excited about learning and constantly nurtured our curiosity. They made going to the library such a big deal that I was boastfully proud when I got my own library card. As a young boy, I developed an insatiable thirst for knowledge.

In that same vein, here in America we need to shift the conversation from one about failing schools and flatlined achievement gaps to one which generates excitement about learning among our children and communities. We need to do a cultural pivot. Everything we say and do about education and learning in America must become aspirational in tone and content. We need an America where learning becomes infectious. We need an America where the models that work, be they public, private, charter, digital, or home schooling, are lifted to higher acclaim. And we need an America where parents and children are at the front of the discussion as opposed to the end of it.

A large part of building this new American education culture requires a conscious effort to take politics out of the education discussion. Our sole focus should be to create a national obsession around learning that transcends the politics of the day. Through this effort, we can develop a new brand of nationalism that has not been witnessed by most Americans.

It is time for us to get excited about the future of education. It is time for us to celebrate what is possible rather than what is not. It is time for a different approach to learning. It is time for us to develop personal and national pride around learning in America. This is my learning manifesto.

Acknowledgments

When I think of my life, the one word that comes to mind is gratitude. I am thankful to have been born to the parents I had and, along with my siblings, was fortunate to have been raised in a household fostered by a love of learning that allowed me to dream big. I am grateful for my vast experiences, the places I have seen, the cultures I have come to know, and the family God has given me. I am also grateful to have found my life's work. From my early professional years of practicing law to my public service as an elected official, my destiny was revealed to me when I focused on the challenges and opportunities associated with the education of our young. I am extremely blessed to do the work I was called to do.

With this book, however, I have come full circle. In unpacking my own educational and political experiences, I now know that we must create a nationwide love of learning—something that cannot be done through education policy, executive, or legislative action. Through community, we *can* build a new culture of learning, and I am grateful to show how we can get there in this book.

I owe a big thanks to my assorted family members who have always supported me and my work in education. I am particularly thankful for the love and support of my amazing life partner, Amber Lewis, and my two incredible sons, Kevin B. Chavous and Eric B. Chavous. And thanks to my fellow board members and the entire American Federation for Children (AFC) team.

Eternal thanks to copyeditor extraordinaire, the gifted Alyssa Devlin, who helped me whip this book into shape and made it flow seamlessly.

Thanks also to the following people who helped me at various stages during the book's development: James Benedict, Ken Campbell, Yvette East, Nakisha Hobbs, Carol Keenan, Kristi Kimball, Matt Latimer, Kim Martinez, Monique Pittman, and Keith Urbahn.

Special thanks to Tom Rooney, Barry Sommer, and the entire Lindsay Unified School District (LUSD) team.

I am so honored to have former US Secretary of Education Dr. Rod Paige write the Foreword to this book. Secretary Paige has been a champion for kids his entire professional career, and his positive impact on learning in America will be felt for years to come. I am privileged to count him as my friend.

Thank you Laila Ali, Deborah Gist, Rick Hess, Denisha Merriweather, Jalen Rose, Dr. Thomas Stewart, and John White for endorsing my book.

Special thanks to Mary Curtis and the entire Transaction Publishers family for continuing to share my education vision with the world.

One final thought: as a boy, I always passionately believed in the power of me—my ability to be whatever I wanted to be, to scale any heights, to accomplish any goal. It almost did not matter if I achieved the goal, because what was most important was my belief that I could. While my parents helped to cultivate that feeling of confidence in me, much of it came from my being in a constant state of learning and growing. That learning and growing fed my confidence and ultimately fueled my life, for which I am so grateful to have. I want all children to have that feeling that I had as a child. If they did, what a wonderful world this would be.

Endorsements

"In *Building a Learning Culture in America*, I really like that Kevin Chavous is talking about how we can make education cool again! Learning is cool, being well-educated is important, and it should be fun! We need to join Kevin in building a national movement around learning."

—Laila Ali, fitness and wellness expert, television personality, and boxing champion

"I had the opportunity to work with Kevin in Washington, DC and saw first-hand his unwavering commitment to the education of our children. *Building a Learning Culture in America* is a story, a reflection, a consideration of national and international education issues, and most importantly, a manifesto. Kevin draws you into his self-described 'life's work' by sharing his personal story and his journey into becoming a vocal, effective and sought-after advocate for children. Whether you agree with all of his stances or not, you will be moved by his passion and touched by the stories he shares of children and schools from around the globe. I'm ready to be a part of Made in America. Let's do it!"

—Deborah Gist, superintendent, Tulsa public schools

"Education often brings to mind the old saying about the weather—everyone talks about it, but no one does anything about it. Kevin Chavous is not everyone. A force of nature himself, he's been battling to reshape American education for two decades. Weaving together educational expertise, lessons from other social movements, and his personal testimonial, he has penned a book that is both manifesto and strategic plan. The result is a remarkable resource for parents, practitioners, and policymakers."

—Frederick M. Hess, director of Education Policy Studies at the American Enterprise Institute

"An absorbing and completely captivating narrative of one man's impact on education in America through the years. Being a former recipient of the Florida Tax-Credit Scholarship, it is encouraging to travel back in time with Kevin as he displays his love for my education and many other low-income children like me. This is a beautiful book and memoir where we can witness how Kevin has fully immersed himself in education reform and how his passion for school reform is contagious. *Building a Learning Culture in America* is a remarkable evolutionary perspective on education reform."

—Denisha Merriweather, MSW candidate at the University of South Florida, former recipient of the Florida Tax Credit Scholarship

"Kevin and I have worked together breaking down barriers to education choice through the American Federation for Children. He is passionate about improving the educational landscape and his new book, *Building a Learning Culture in America*, provides thoughtful insight on how to get education back on track."

—Jalen Rose, ESPN analyst, former NBA star, and founder of the Jalen Rose Leadership Academy

"*Building a Learning Culture in America* demonstrates Kevin Chavous' unique combination of personal experiences, professional expertise, and unwavering commitment to ensuring all children receive a quality education. Chavous reminds us that instilling a life-long love and appreciation for learning in all young people is the most significant responsibility we have as adults. I encourage anyone interested in understanding the root causes of academic underachievement, as well as a viable strategy to improve outcomes for all America's children, to read this book."

—Dr. Thomas Stewart, president of Patten University

"Amidst the jargon of education policy and the bitterness of education politics, we can forget the simple moral imperative to improve our schools and the abundant evidence that it is possible, for all children in all neighborhoods. Tying his personal evolution to the success stories that inspired his views, Kevin Chavous provides clear prescriptions for building a national consciousness of educational inequality. A member of the progressive establishment unafraid to push even the progressive paradigm, Chavous calls us to think independently about an issue characterized by intransigence and entrenchment."

—John White, Louisiana
State superintendent of education

Introduction

The Attorney General's eyes were blazing with anger, hostility, and murderous intent. And they were glaring straight at me as he purposefully walked my way. I had just greeted and hugged Eric Holder's wife, Dr. Sharon Malone, but I could tell by the look on her husband's face that he was not looking to hug me. He looked more like he wanted to hit me.

It was 2009, and I had just finished an enjoyable evening at the Thelonious Monk Institute of Jazz competition at the Kennedy Center. The institute has been operating for many years, and one of its highlights is to give a scholarship to a young performing artist who stands out among the many other youth performances. The event also features performances by the very best jazz musicians in the world. A friend had invited me to attend, and the evening was wonderful until I saw Attorney General Holder marching toward me.

My friend and I were viewing the program from one of the Kennedy Center box seats. About fifteen other people were in our section. Eric Holder and his wife, Dr. Sharon Malone, were in the box seat section next to ours, which also contained about fifteen people. Both sections had to exit out of the same door. It was as my friend and I were walking out that we noticed Sharon. Sharon greeted us both warmly and the three of us were engaged in small talk when I saw Eric coming our way with about three to four secret service agents in tow.

"Kevin," he yelled, "you need to leave MY president alone! You need to back off of those commercials criticizing him about the DC voucher program. Just stop it!"

The Attorney General was yelling so loud that the thirty or so people trying to exit just stopped and began staring at me. The secret service agents were all frowning my way. Sharon and my friend were aghast. Both took a step back from me. But I was ready.

"Eric," I began, "He is not YOUR president, he is OUR president and you need to tell OUR president that he needs to do the right thing. He needs to do what's best for our children. That program works. Over 90 percent of the students are graduating from high school and going to college. And they come from schools where 85 percent of the students are failing. For the life of me, Eric, I can't understand why the president is trying to shut down a program that is a lifeline for parents and children from our worse schools. Some of those children from southeast DC will be in class with Sasha and Malia at Sidwell Friends and he wants to shut it down? I am not backing away, Eric. Tell President Obama to do the right thing—for our children!"

By then, I had many of the crowd with me. The hostility in their faces was gone. While I was making my points, I even noticed that a couple of the secret service agents were nodding with me. That emboldened me more. By the time I finished, I was yelling as loud as Eric was when he first accosted me.

"Just stop it, Kevin," the Attorney General said, lowering the tone of his voice. I could tell that he knew that his demeanor was not very Attorney General-like. Plus Sharon was giving him those "calm down" looks.

"You just need to stop it," he said, even more softly.

By now, everyone had taken a deep breath. The tension has eased considerably.

"Eric, I have a lot of respect for you, but I will continue to fight for these children, even if I have to fight President Obama."

I did understand why Eric Holder was angry with me. Along with Eric and about twenty other prominent African-American men in DC, we hosted a major fundraiser for then Senator Barack Obama and raised several hundred thousand dollars in one night. During the campaign I was on Senator Obama's education policy committee. I went to the inaugural balls and was on the team, not an insider, but on the team. But I was also past the point of going along to get along in my life. I was on a mission. I couldn't sleep at night knowing that some children would wake up the next morning and, through no fault of their own, go to bad schools. And everyone is ok with that? Well, not me. Soon after he was elected, President Obama decided that he was going to shut down the highly successful

DC Opportunity Scholarship Program (DCOSP). The program provided public scholarship money for low-income families in DC to send their children to participating private schools in DC. Many of the highly regarded Catholic schools participated: schools like Gonzaga, St. John's, and Archbishop Carroll. Other more exclusive schools like Sidwell Friends and Georgetown Prep also participated. Those schools all loved the program so much that they accepted the children even though the $7,500 scholarship didn't come close to covering the tuition. The schools gifted the balance. The teachers union hated the program, just like they hated charter schools. But for the life of me, I couldn't understand why the president wouldn't support it, nor could I fathom why he and his Education Secretary Arne Duncan immediately rescinded the acceptance letters to 216 children who had received notice of their scholarships right after the president was sworn into office. Several of those children were from Ward 7, the ward I had represented on the DC Council. All of the families with acceptance letters were devastated by Obama's decision to snatch their children's scholarships. One family in far southeast did, indeed, have a little girl who was slated to go to Sidwell Friends and actually be in class with one of Obama's daughters. Right after the family got the news of the scholarship, they saw the new First Lady on television talking about hosting White House sleepovers for Sasha and Malia's classmates. That family from southeast was so excited that they borrowed money to buy clothes for their daughter so she could be ready for a potential White House visit. They were crushed soon thereafter when they received Secretary Duncan's letter rescinding the scholarship.

Although I had been out of office since 2005, I was immersed in the national education reform and educational choice movement. I was on several national education reform boards, including the Black Alliance for Educational Options (BAEO). Working with BAEO and local parents like Virginia Walden Ford, I began to organize rallies, protests, and letters to try to get the president to change his mind. We ran bus ads, television ads, and even a full-page ad—an open letter to the president that I signed—in the *New York Times*. I even got former DC mayor, Anthony Williams, to cosign an op-ed I wrote which appeared in the *Washington Post*. Despite all of our efforts, the president wouldn't budge. He had made his deal with the teachers union. That night at the Kennedy Center, the Attorney General was just expressing the frustration felt by the administration about someone like me (a member of the club) not falling in line. For me, however, this issue transcended the politics of the day. It was my life's work.

Driving home past the monuments and the tidal basin, I thought about the president, Eric Holder, and that family in southeast DC. I wished to myself that I had told Eric more about that girl and her family. But it wouldn't have made a difference. They had their political priorities, and those priorities had nothing to do with the dreams or aspirations of a poor kid and her family in southeast DC. I also thought about my time on the Council of the District of Columbia and my advocacy for educational choice. I reflected on the protests at my house and the hecklers. Then I thought about my father, and I laughed. Dad was right: no one who has done anything for their fellow man was cheered while they were doing it. I sure wasn't being cheered by Eric Holder. But that's ok, because I was doing what I thought was right, fighting to get all of our children a quality education—by any means necessary. If he were still with us, my dad would get it and support me every step of the way. He passionately believed that education was the great equalizer, the ticket to a productive life. He instilled that thinking in my three siblings and me. My belief in the power of education and learning was unshakeable. It always has been, right from the very beginning. Which is why, after my years of experience and exposure in the world of education in DC and throughout America, I have decided to share my story. I have broken this book into three parts. The first part shares my personal history of education, my journey as a DC councilmember, and the convictions I gained as chair of the education committee. In the second part, I dive into the solutions I see as the best path forward for education today, and in the third part I highlight some examples of institutions and approaches that have succeeded, that have built unique learning cultures. I hope that in its telling, this book will not only educate readers, but inspire them as well.

Part 1

The Politics of Reform—My Struggle for School Choice

1

My Personal History of Learning

I remember it like it was yesterday: my first day of school. I was so excited. When my mother woke me up that day, my three younger siblings were still asleep. That made me feel like the oldest. I felt responsible and special to be the first to go to school. Both of my parents had made a big deal about me starting school. My father's mother, Grandma Emma, even traveled to Indianapolis from Aiken just for my first day. After I woke up, I ate cereal and put on a blue button-down shirt, gray corduroy pants, and new black Thom McAn shoes. Grandma Emma had brought me a brand new gray sweater, which she surprised me with after I got dressed. My father told me to pay attention to my teacher and my mom started to cry. I got a hug from Grandma Emma and walked out the door, with each of my parents holding one of my hands as we started to walk the two and a half blocks to James Whitcomb Riley School 43 in northwest Indianapolis.

I was ready for my first day of kindergarten.

For me, as a five-year-old entering school in Indianapolis during the early 1960s, I was very happy to be going to school. Little did I know at the time, but I was being raised in a household that contained its own learning culture. My father, Harold P. Chavous, had been the first in his family to attend college, having graduated from South Carolina State University with a degree in chemistry. He grew up on a farm in Aiken, South Carolina, and by the time he was nine years old, his mother Emma, Aunt Rose, and Great Uncle Pa Bradley all agreed that young HP was more suited for schooling than farmwork. So they allowed him to walk seven miles each way to a one-room school house. Before long, he was helping the teacher teach other children numbers and reading. At fifteen, he enrolled in South Carolina State. After graduating, HP joined the army, served in Korea, and met my mother, Bettie Jane Lowery, while stationed in Indiana. After the war, my father enrolled in medical school, but had to drop out after two years when my siblings and I were born. He later enrolled in Butler University's pharmacy school and became one of the first black licensed pharmacists in the state.

My mother also valued education. Her father was one of the only black physicians in Indianapolis, and she attended Butler University as well. As a young boy, I would watch them read all kinds of books and talk about the things they read. I distinctly remember sitting on the floor, playing with my Tonka truck, and longing for the day when I could read with them and join them in discussing all that they had read. So, understandably, I was proud and smiling that entire first day of school.

My love of learning was further developed in first grade, thanks to my wonderful teacher, Helen Shelton. Ms. Shelton was the first person outside of my nuclear family who made me feel like I was smart and special. Ms. Shelton applauded me for anything and everything. "My, Kevin, I really like the way you did your alphabet today," she would say with a smile. "You are so smart!" Or, "Kevin, I just love the way you print and the way you hold your pencil. You are going to be such a good writer." And even when I refused to put the crayons back in the box the right way, she would celebrate my independence. "You know, Kevin, your way of organizing this box of crayons may be better than the people who made them. They are all so neat! I am so proud of you." By the time I finished first grade, I believed two things: that I was the smartest person in the world and that I could be anything that I wanted to be. Of course, the act of instilling self-confidence in a young student by itself doesn't guarantee future academic success. But for many children—particularly young boys of color—early elementary school years exacerbate emerging insecurities and feelings of academic inferiority. As for me, I benefited greatly from Helen Shelton's nurturing and encouraging approach. In fact, early in life my confidence and belief in myself, which was boosted by my desire to learn, led me to believe I could solve problems and make a difference. It helped that I lived in the racially diverse Butler Tarkington neighborhood of Indianapolis and attended St. Thomas Aquinas, a great elementary school.

Now that I have traveled all over the country and intimately know at least twenty major cities, I can really appreciate the Butler Tarkington neighborhood of the 1960s and 1970s. In spite of the racial and generational turbulence of the day, that community was extremely tolerant. At St. Thomas, the racial mix of white and African-American students was about 65 to 35 percent. My mother was very active in all of my school activities, and it felt as though parental involvement was encouraged at the school. The teachers and staff at the school did a very good job of treating everyone the same. Incredibly I never experienced any racial prejudice at the school, something I was to face with regularity in high school and college. I loved St. Thomas. I don't know how they did it, but in choosing that school, my parents found the perfect fit for me.

The combination of good parenting, great teachers, and continual encouragement created in me a can-do mindset, the feeling that I could get things done. Interestingly, the summer before I started high school, I did do something pretty unique: I helped to start a public park.

As a boy, I always did well in sports. And though I eventually settled on basketball as my preferred sport while in high school, baseball was my first love, and I was a good football player as well. My neighborhood friends and I played baseball and football for hours on end on a two-acre lot that bordered my backyard near Butler University. A giant water tower was in the middle of the lot, but we had more than enough room to throw passes or hit baseballs—well, for the most part. One day, while we were playing baseball, someone hit the ball near the water tower and almost hit the water company worker who had been checking on the tower. He angrily threw the ball back at us, saying, "You children are going to have to find somewhere else to play when they sell this land to build houses on it." Me and my best friend, Bryan Williams, then went to talk to the man to find out what he meant. He informed us that the water company leaders and the park staff had been trying to decide what to do with the land, but that it looked like both sides were inclined to sell it to be developed.

A couple of days later, Bryan and I took a bus downtown to meet with the city parks' director—unscheduled. Since he was busy, we had to wait for a couple of hours. When he finally saw us, he confirmed what the water company employee had told us. He also said that some people wanted the land to become an official park, but there was a concern about whether it would get much usage. Bryan and I told him that we play there every day and that we knew at least twenty children who would play there if there were swing sets and a play area for younger children. He looked at us long and hard. I could tell he was sizing us up. Who wouldn't? He had two fourteen-year-olds in his office asking him to save a park on land ripe for development. He said, "If you get me signatures from the parents of those children, along with the types of activities that would work there, I will recommend that we turn it into a park."

Bryan and I went to work. Little did I know, this was my first grassroots campaign. We knocked on doors, talked to parents, and got around fifty signatures from our neighborhood. We also had secured several letters from our neighbors saying that they would rather have a park at that site than more houses.

The park director was stunned. Within a few weeks, just before the start of summer, Water Tower Park officially opened. I was fourteen years old, and I had helped to start a brand new city park.

After leaving St. Thomas, I went to Brebeuf Preparatory High School, then an all-male Jesuit school in Indianapolis. Brebeuf was a terrific school and the perfect fit for me. I intuitively connected with the Jesuit belief in service for the benefit of others. My high-school years were full of volunteer work. In fact, it seemed like all I did was work. By then, my father had opened Chavous Drugs in near northeast Indianapolis. It was a true family business. I would sweep and mop the floors, stock the shelves, refill the soda machine, and deliver prescriptions. My sisters, Estella and Rose, would work the cash register, and my brother Edwin, the youngest, would fill in where needed. Doing the prescription deliveries allowed me to fully experience empathy for others. I used to make most of my deliveries at a couple of senior apartment buildings. After a while, I noticed that some of the seniors on my regular delivery stops would be dressed up when I arrived. Still others would have cakes, pies, and sometimes even full meals prepared for me. I would sometimes stop and engage with these elderly ladies, but I was usually in a rush since I wanted to make sure I finished all of the deliveries. At one point, I mentioned it to my father, complaining about how long it was taking me to do my deliveries. He said, "Son, I know it is time consuming, but you see how much time I take with some of these customers? A lot of folks need that and the seniors you take those prescriptions to are, for the most part, sick and shut in. Don't you see? You are the only contact many of those seniors have. You are their lifeline. Just try to leave a little earlier and take the time you can with each of them." In his own way, my dad was a "cause" guy too. But more significantly, my learning and growing was helping to shape and guide me toward my future in public service.

2

A Look at Education in America

The Creation of an Education System "*For All*"

Once upon a time, America had a learning culture unlike any in the history of mankind. Thomas Jefferson planted the seed for public education believing that the only way democracy could survive was by having an educated citizenry who appreciated the duties and responsibilities of citizenship, and that as a nation, we had to inculcate certain values and mores in our children.[1] To make this work, Jefferson recommended dividing Virginia into several wards, or "hundreds," each with a primary school providing free instruction to the area's children in reading, writing, and geography.[2] Later, between 1830 and 1860, designs were being developed to put in place state systems of public education. In the 1840s, Massachusetts Secretary of Education Horace Mann championed the Prussian model of common schools which divided students according to age, taught those students basically the same content irrespective of their various aptitudes, and adopted the stand-and-deliver lecture approach, which resulted in students being passive recipients of information rather than active participants in the learning process. These schools also adopted a 9 AM to 3 PM school day, with summers off, which followed the agricultural needs at the time. Mann was hailed for his approach, which focused on public school education for all, taught by professional teachers.[3] By 1918, all states had compulsory attendance laws.[4] This was during the progressive era, which ushered in a new age of wealth and prosperity in America. In the nation's growing cities, the lure of jobs, factory growth, and higher wages contributed to more and more people becoming city dwellers. America was changing into an urban nation. That change also affected schools and our approach to education. For

9

progressive era disciples, a primary goal of progressive education was to make schools more effective agencies of a democratic society. As described by Beavercreek Schools:

> Schools have changed throughout America's history as the nation has changed from frontier and rural to industrialized and increasingly technologically sophisticated. A major shift in educational practices came during the early 1900s when third grade reading, writing, and arithmetic became inadequate preparation for an increasingly complex society. The educational experiments from this period are known as "progressive reforms," taking their name from the "progressive era" in American education.[5]

The progressives all shared the conviction that democracy meant being actively involved in social, political, and economic decisions that could affect each individual.[6] As the nation was growing more urban and sophisticated, the progressives wanted to ensure that citizens were engaged in all aspects of political and economic decision making. Also during this era, as public education became more formalized and universal, "normal schools" became more prevalent. "Normal school" was a phrase given to institutions built for the training of teachers. In the late nineteenth century, as public schools became more formalized and universal, there was a growing demand for teachers. As a result, the proliferation of normal schools occurred. By the twentieth century, most states had at least one normal school and most cities with large populations had a normal school tied to a specific high school. Later, as normal schools morphed into four-year colleges and eventually state universities, established state universities that did not already have them began to develop teacher preparation programs. University and college teacher education programs grew rapidly as states developed specific licensure requirements often based on college-level coursework.[7] The upshot of all of these developments is that the United States was shaping a system with the purpose of educating its children as competently as possible in order to keep up with the skilled job demands flowing from the industrial revolution.[8]

The results were staggering. From 1910 to 1940, the US high-school graduation rate rose from 9 to 50 percent.[9] With such a great change, America was quickly becoming a world leader in education.[10]

The United States embraced teaching techniques established by Horace Mann in the early 1800s—such as the teaching of widely applicable skills that were not specific to certain careers or geographic locations. The skills that were taught were intended to be transferable across the increasingly diverse American economy. However, within this overarching structure of variety, the American school system allowed for individual regions to decide the curriculum and oversee the day-to-day schooling.[11]

In reality, America developed a learning culture through committing to the power and promise of educational opportunities for all, an ideal consistent with the American belief that anyone who worked hard could reach their full potential, no matter what their background.

However, things were not as equal and opportunity was not immediately as widespread as it sounds. The American ideal I describe above had unspoken caveats attached to it, and our failure to hold true to the promise of an education for all helped undermine the very people the system was designed to serve. For instance, African Americans and other minorities were not considered in the growing American learning culture, an exclusion which ultimately helped spawn the civil rights movement.[12]

Many people don't know that the civil rights movement in America got its legs through the area of education. Early in the twentieth century, during the period of "separate but equal" as defined in the Supreme Court case that made segregation legal in America, *Plessy v. Ferguson*, it became clear exactly how unequal education was, particularly for blacks and those of lower socioeconomic status.[13] As a result, many of the advances developed during the Progressive Era were ultimately illusory: they were designed for the elite and some poor whites. For the most part, far too many of the masses were left out of the equation. When Thurgood Marshall joined the NAACP Legal Defense Fund, his work really ignited the fire that led to the civil rights movement of the 1950s and 1960s. Marshall would file lawsuits in places like Texas, Oklahoma, and Virginia to challenge the separate but equal doctrine and would argue that every American child should have equal access to a quality education. After years of strategic legal maneuvering and aggressive litigation, Marshall argued and won *Brown v. Board of*

Education, the landmark case that overturned *Plessy v. Ferguson* and legally outlawed segregation in America. The *Brown* court held that:

> the doctrine of "separate but equal" has no place. Separate educational facilities are inherently unequal. Therefore, we hold that the plaintiffs and others similarly situated for whom the actions have been brought are, by reason of the segregation complained of, deprived of the equal protection of the laws guaranteed by the Fourteenth Amendment.[14]

Even as some of these inconsistencies were being addressed by the Supreme Court decision of *Brown v. Board of Education* and the resulting civil rights movement of the 1960s, many of America's local school districts became pawns in limiting access to good schools for low-income children of color.

The aftermath of the *Brown* decision brought about blatant resistance from a host of governors and political segregationists. Texas Attorney General John Ben Shepperd organized a campaign to generate legal obstacles to the implementation of desegregation.[15]

In 1957, Arkansas Governor Orval Faubus blocked nine black students from entering Little Rock Central High School, an action which led President Eisenhower to deploy the 101st Airborne Division from Fort Campbell, Kentucky, to Arkansas and federalize Arkansas's National Guard. The students became forever known as the Little Rock Nine.[16]

Also in 1957, Florida's response was mixed. Its legislature passed an Interposition Resolution denouncing the decision and declaring it null and void. But Florida Governor LeRoy Collins, though joining in the protest against the court decision, refused to sign it, arguing that the attempt to overturn the ruling must be done by legal methods.[17]

In 1963, Alabama Governor George Wallace personally blocked the door to Foster Auditorium at the University of Alabama to prevent the enrollment of two black students. This became the infamous "Stand in the Schoolhouse Door," where Wallace personally backed his "segregation now, segregation tomorrow, segregation forever" policy that he had stated in his 1963 inaugural address. He moved aside only when confronted by General Henry Graham of the Alabama National Guard, who was ordered by President John F. Kennedy to intervene. Wallace became one of the more enduring symbols of racism during the civil rights movement of the 1960s.[18]

But possibly the most diabolical and insidious response came from Virginia.

Virginia Senator Harry F. Byrd, Sr., organized the Massive Resistance movement that included the closing of schools rather than desegregating them. Because *Brown* did not apply to private schools, the founding of new private academies in the 1950s, 1960s, and 1970s emerged as a way for whites to practice segregation. These academies began to pop up all over the south, but Virginia was one of the first, and they took the concept to a whole new level. Several Virginia counties shut down their public schools and then reappropriated the dollars into scholarships only for white children to attend these newfound white academies. After much legal back and forth between the counties and the federal government, most of the counties had to cease these practices. But Prince Edward County was different and took even longer to desegregate.[19]

The county's board refused to appropriate any money to operate the schools, which chose to close rather than comply with the federal desegregation order. It was the only school district in the country to resort to such extreme measures. White students took advantage of state tuition vouchers to attend segregation academies, but black students had no education alternatives within the county. Finally, in 1963, Prince Edwards' schools were ordered to open, and when the Supreme Court agreed to hear the county's appeal, supervisors gave in rather than risk prison. Then, in 1964, the US Supreme Court decided on *Griffin v. County School Board of Prince Edward County*, and segregationists could appeal no longer.[20] However, when Prince Edward County's schools finally opened, many of the African-American children hadn't been in school for over two years. Some never recovered, leaving some to refer to the black children of Prince Edward County as the crippled generation.[21]

One clear result of the civil rights movement was a more focused effort by the federal government to enforce *Brown*. At the time of the *Brown* decision, seventeen states and the District of Columbia had laws requiring that schools be segregated.[22] Federal judges were now overseeing plans to desegregate the public schools in all of those states. To accelerate the effort, the practice of taking children out of their neighborhood school and busing them to other schools in order to integrate those schools became popular. Nobody liked busing. Black children met hostility when bused to a white school and vice versa. During the 1970s, it all came to a head. Parents were regularly protesting and mini riots were popping up all over. Schools were no longer fun—it was tough to be passionate about learning when you were fearful of your safety throughout the school day.

Busing impacted everyone involved. For the students being bused, they knew that they were entering a hostile situation in which they knew that the people at the new school would not like them, even though they had never met them. For the children at the receiving school, they were being told by parents, teachers, and administrators that busing was not a good thing, so those children were often conflicted about how they felt. It did not help things when many of the children saw their parents joining protests, throwing objects at buses, and booing as the new children exited the bus. Was busing worth it? Well, it worked for some of the children, but all were scarred. The physical and emotional toll on the nation was hard, especially on the heels of the turbulent 1960s. And how about the ultimate end goal? Wasn't busing supposed to be the catalyst to integrate America's schools? Indeed, that did not happen. Today's America is more segregated than it was at the time busing began, a painful illustration of the impacts associated with trying to force people to do something that they do not want to do.[23] Ultimately, while our nation was built with an idyllic view of education and progress, it couldn't fully succeed when it was limiting the benefits of education to only one group within the entire population. While *Brown* knocked the old mentality on its side, the backlash that accompanied the civil rights movement stunted equal access to education for years to come. This struggle was further exacerbated by a lack of attention and focus on school systems in the 1960s and 1970s.

1960s and 1970s: In the Midst of Great Change, Our Schools Remained Stagnant

The civil rights movement and ensuing political activism of the 1960s and 1970s advanced freedom and ultimately changed America for the better. Those decades, however, did not advance education and learning for American schoolchildren. If anything, all of the turmoil and strife of the time negatively impacted teachers and students alike. The so-called remedies like court-imposed busing certainly did not help.

And the white flight from our cities during this time also led to a bunker mentality adopted by our upper middle and elite class. They worked hard to create their own educational oasis for their children through carefully insulated public and private schools. Largely for cosmetic purposes, these upper middle class and wealthy Americans eventually allowed selected children of color and other low-income white children into their closely protected schools. This "creaming" created a huge strain for many of our local public school districts and the result was clear: most urban school districts eventually consisted of low-income children from the most challenging backgrounds with limited parental or educator support.

Before long, our nation's gradual slide in the K-12 education of our young was becoming more and more apparent. Sadly, the accumulated years of struggle over who was entitled to be educated (and how) contributed mightily to the overall decline of our education system, one which had once been the envy of the world. While America was trying to get its social house in order, it was ignoring the basic need to foster creativity and innovation in education. The impact of that reality would haunt us for decades.

Notes

1. *Thomas Jefferson: Creating a Virginia Republic*, The Library of Congress Online, accessed December 29, 2015, http://www.loc.gov/exhibits/jefferson/jeffrep.html. In this online exhibit, under *The Role of Education*, the Library of Congress highlights a document in which Jefferson declares that "well-informed people can be trusted with self-government".

2. Thomas Jefferson, *Notes on the State of Virginia*, 268, University of Virginia Library Online, accessed December 29, 2015, http://search.lib.virginia.edu/catalog/uva-lib:710304/view#openLayer/uva-lib:1195571/2486/1821/1/1/0.

3. Lawrence A. Cremin, *The Republic and the School: Horace Mann On the Education of Free Men* (New York: Teachers College, 1957), 21–23.

4. Michael Katz, *A History of Compulsory Education Laws, Fastback Series No 75. Bicentennial Series* (Bloomington, IN: Phi Delta Kappa, 1976), 18.

5. *Educational Reforms from the Early 1900's*, Beavercreek Schools Unofficial Web Page, accessed December 29, 2015, http://personalweb.donet.com/~eprice/fare.htm#nmsaovrv.

6. *A Brief Overview of Progressive Education*, The Dewey Project on Progressive Education at University of Vermont, accessed December 29, 2015, http://www.uvm.edu/~dewey/articles/proged.html.
7. Christine D. Myers, as cited by Christopher G. Bates, *The Early Republic and Antebellum America: An Encyclopedia of Social, Political, Cultural, and Economic History* (New York: Routledge, 2015), 317.
8. Michael Katz, *A History of Compulsory Education Laws, Fastback Series No 75. Bicentennial Series.* (Bloomington, IN: Phi Delta Kappa, 1976), 14.
9. Goldin, Claudia, and Lawrence F. Katz, "Human Capital and Social Capital: The Rise of Secondary Schooling in America, 1910–1940," *Journal of Interdisciplinary History* 29, no. 4(1999): 683–723.
10. Goldin, Claudia, "The Human-Capital Century and American Leadership: Virtues of the Past,"*Journal of Economic History* 61, no. 2 (2001): 263–90.
11. Ellwood P. Cubberley, *Public Education in the United States* (Cambridge: Houghton Mifflin, 1919), 167.
12. *School Desegregation and Equal Educational Opportunity*, Leadership Conference on Civil Rights Education, accessed December 29, 2015, http://www.civilrights.org/resources/civilrights101/desegregation.html.
13. Plessy v. Ferguson, 163 U.S. 537 (1896).
14. Brown v. Board of Education of Topeka, 347 U.S. 483 (1954).
15. Mark C. Howell, "John Ben Shepperd, Attorney General of the State of Texas: His Role in the Continuation of Segregation in Texas, 1953–1957," Master's Thesis, The University of Texas of the Permian Basin, Odessa, Texas, July 2003.
16. *The History Behind the Little Rock Nine*, State of Arkansas Official Website, accessed December 29, 2015, http://www.arkansas.com/attractions/central-high/.
17. *Interposition Resolution by the Florida Legislature in Response to Brown v. Board of Education, 1957, with Handwritten Note by Florida Governor LeRoy Collins*, the World Digital Library, last updated October 17, 2014, http://www.wdl.org/en/item/14196/.
18. *Wallace in the Schoolhouse Door: Marking the 40th Anniversary of Alabama's Civil Rights Standoff*, National Public Radio Online, accessed December 29, 2015, http://www.npr.org/2003/06/11/1294680/wallace-in-the-schoolhouse-door.
19. *Brown at 60: The Southern Manifesto and "Massive Resistance" to Brown*, NAACP Legal Defense and Educational Fund, accessed December 29, 2015, http://www.naacpldf.org/brown-at-60-southern-manifesto-and-massive-resistance-brown.
20. Griffin et al. v. County School Board of Prince Edward County et al., 377 U.S. 218 (1964).
21. *Separate Is Not Equal, Brown v. Board of Education: Five Communities since* Brown, Smithsonian National Museum of American History Online, accessed December 29, 2015, http://americanhistory.si.edu/brown/history/6-legacy/five-since-brown.html.
22. *Segregation's Citadel Unbreached in 4 Years*, Washington Observer, Sunday, May 11, 1958. Newspaper map. Geography and Map Division, Library

of Congress Online, accessed December 29, 2015, https://www.loc.gov/exhibits/brown/brown-aftermath.html.

23. "Report: Public schools more segregated now than 40 years ago," *Washington Post* Online, August 29, 2013, https://www.washingtonpost.com/news/answer-sheet/wp/2013/08/29/report-public-schools-more-segregated-now-than-40-years-ago/.

3

A Nation at Risk:
Then and Now

A Nation at Risk

The opening preamble to the landmark 1983 report, *A Nation at Risk*, reads as follows:

> Our Nation is at risk. Our once unchallenged preeminence in commerce, industry, science, and technological innovation is being overtaken by competitors throughout the world. This report is concerned with only one of the many causes and dimensions of the problem, but it is the one that undergirds American prosperity, security, and civility. We report to the American people that while we can take justifiable pride in what our schools and colleges have historically accomplished and contributed to the United States and the well-being of its people, the educational foundations of our society are presently being eroded by a rising tide of mediocrity that threatens our very future as a Nation and a people. What was unimaginable a generation ago has begun to occur—others are matching and surpassing our educational attainments.
>
> If an unfriendly foreign power had attempted to impose on America the mediocre educational performance that exists today, we might well have viewed it as an act of war. As it stands, we have allowed this to happen to ourselves. We have even squandered the gains in student achievement made in the wake of the Sputnik challenge. Moreover, we have dismantled essential support systems which helped make those gains possible. We have, in effect, been committing an act of unthinking, unilateral educational disarmament.[1]

Strong words. And the report is even stronger, more damning, more prescient than one would expect, particularly given the time it was released. The year 1983 was the early part of the Reagan years. It was a time when President Ronald Reagan boldly put pride back into what it meant to be an American. I certainly didn't agree with many of his policies, but it is undeniable that he led the country away from the malaise that engulfed the Jimmy Carter presidency. Knowing that, it would seem all the more unlikely that Reagan would appoint a commission charged with the task of examining our education system, only to have that commission castigate nearly every aspect of our K-12 approach.

Some have suggested that the commission was a modern version of the red scare tactics of the 1950s in which American propaganda about Soviet domination fueled the Cold War. But a critical review of *A Nation at Risk* report tells another story. It told the truth.

Within each of the categories of recommendations, the commission makes detailed suggestions. Over thirty years later, virtually none of the thirty-eight recommendations have been adopted, and we have consistently continued our decline as a world leader in the educational attainment of our people.[2]

Others, however, have viewed the report as a heavy critique of teachers and an overblown assault on public education. To those critics, the report inaugurated a series of attacks on public schools. "That was the 'rising tide' we got engulfed with—the rising tide of negative reports," said Paul Houston, former executive director of the American Association of School Administrators and a former Princeton, New Jersey public schools superintendent. "It was an overstatement of the problem, and it led to sort of hysterical responses," he said on the twenty-fifth anniversary of the report's release, adding that it also led to "a cottage industry of national reports by people saying how bad things are."[3] Still, the famed American Federation of Teachers leader, Albert Shanker, embraced the recommendations, according to his biographer Richard Kahlenberg.[4] And even public school advocate Diane Ravitch called it "most important education reform document of the 20th century."[5] Interestingly, the one teacher who served on the commission, Jay Sommers, said twenty-five years later that the harsh rhetoric was needed. "Any reasonable teacher should have understood at the time—and I did—that we need to tighten up that belt. We have to *do* something," Sommers said.[6]

Partly as a result of the report, the 1980s became a time of internal school district reform initiatives. Schools were reorganized, reconfigured, reconstituted, consolidated, closed, and retrofitted. Nearly every state had a blue ribbon panel or state commission to review and report on the quality of education in their state.[7] Critics of these reform initiatives point to the report as instigating that policy shift. Also during this time, education school district budgets skyrocketed. Federal spending on education went from $14 billion in 1980 to $67 billion in 2007.[8] While all of this sounds like it could be a positive change, it resulted in a too many cooks in the kitchen scenario that led to too many crossed wires, too much politicking, and not enough done on behalf of our children. In most jurisdictions, school boards are responsible for setting general policies and hiring a superintendent who individually is tasked with making decisions on specific matters such as personnel, construction, and procurement. Many school boards, however, got involved in virtually every nitty-gritty detail, thereby encouraging backroom politics and the opportunity for mischief. Add to the mix the teachers union's powerful resistance to change, and it is easy to understand how the authority of many school district superintendents was compromised.

Of course, not all was this bad and the nation has had sterling examples of school districts that work well. But generally in those positive instances the local superintendent has been able to navigate around the education politics of the day and the various machinations of probing board members. More money.More power. More bureaucracy. It is undeniable that even after all the states' renewed focus on education, the proficiency standing of our children either flatlined or, in many cases, declined, making the case for a belief that I have held for years: that no school bureaucracy will ever reform itself from within. Reform can only occur from outside pressure.

For me, having worked to reform education for nearly twenty years, it is mind-boggling to think that nearly each and every word found in *A Nation at Risk* report and its subsequent recommendations could still be immediately applied to education in America today. Few objective observers would deny that point. If there ever were a time for a pivot in our approach, it is now. We've waited thirty years; let's not wait another thirty to change what needs to be changed.

The raw truth as to where we are today with education in America is that little has changed since 1983's *A Nation at Risk*. If the report's authors were updating their report to reflect the current state of American education, many facts would stay the same and the following facts might well encompass additional indicators of risk:

- Every forty-two seconds, a child drops out of school—that's over two thousand children per day and over seven hundred and fifty thousand children per year.[9]
- While graduation rates have risen to their highest ever (the national graduation rate reached 82 percent in 2013–14), college and career readiness remains low, with fewer than 40 percent of high-school seniors being college-ready.[10]
- As of 2011, nearly half of America's public schools were deemed failing schools.[11]
- Over 30 percent of African-American boys who do drop out spend some time in prison by the time they reach their mid-thirties.[12]

As these statistics show, we are in many ways in no better position than we were thirty years ago, and today we also have research showing that the impact of our stagnancy is not only bad for our children, but also crippling our economy.

The Economic Impact of the Achievement Gap in America's Schools

In 2009 the global management consulting firm McKinsey & Co conducted the first in-depth analysis of the economic impact of the achievement gap on America. The report, titled *The Economic Impact of the Achievement Gap in America's Schools*,[13] represented the first time that our educational shortfalls were quantified economically. While most people are aware of the racial achievement gap—the gap in the educational proficiency of African-American and Hispanic students compared to their white counterparts—McKinsey also addressed three other distinct achievement gap areas: the income achievement gap, the gap between students coming from different household incomes; the systems-based achievement gap, the gap between students enrolled in different school systems or regions; and the economically damaging international achievement gap, the gap between the United States and other nations. In the report's introduction, the McKinsey team states:

> This report finds that the underutilization of human potential in the United States is extremely costly. For individuals, our results show that:
>
> • Avoidable shortfalls in academic achievement impose heavy and often tragic consequences, via lower earnings, poorer health, and higher rates of incarceration.
> • For many students (but by no means all), lagging achievement evidenced as early as fourth grade appears to be a powerful predictor of rates of high school and college graduation, as well as lifetime earnings.
>
> For the economy as a whole, our results show that:
>
> • If the United States had in recent years closed the gap between its educational achievement levels and those of better-performing nations such as Finland and Korea, GDP in 2008 could have been $1.3 trillion to $2.3 trillion higher. This represents 9 to 16 percent of GDP.

NAEP test scores, average for reading and math, 2007
% of students at the "advanced" level

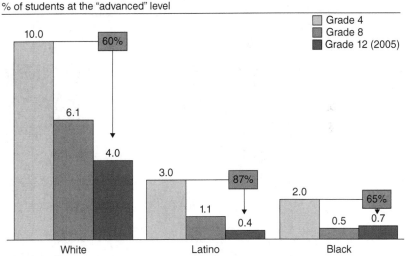

Few black and latino students score at the "advanced" level, and the percentage declines over time

Note: in some cases the number of black and latino students at the "advanced" level was statistically insignificant

Source: USDOE,NCES, National Assessment of Educational progress (NAEP) Summary Data Tables
II. US Census Bureau, "*An older and more diverse Nation by Midcentury*," press release (August 14, 2008)

- If the gap between black and Latino student performance and white student performance had been similarly narrowed, GDP in 2008 would have been between $310 billion and $525 billion higher, or 2 to 4 percent of GDP. The magnitude of this impact will rise in the years ahead as demographic shifts result in blacks and Latinos becoming a larger proportion of the population and workforce.
- If the gap between low-income students and the rest had been similarly narrowed, GDP in 2008 would have been $400 billion to $670 billion higher, or 3 to 5 percent of GDP.
- If the gap between America's low-performing states and the rest had been similarly narrowed, GDP in 2008 would have been $425 billion to $700 billion higher, or 3 to 5 percent of GDP.

Put differently, the persistence of these educational achievement gaps imposes on the United States the economic equivalent of a permanent national recession.

School spending cost-effectiveness
$ in cumulative spending per student per point on PISA mathematics, 2003

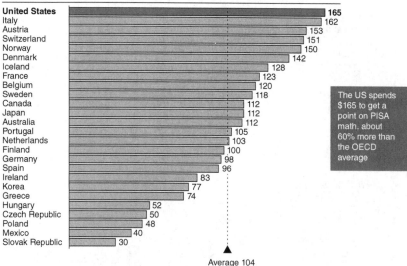

United States	165
Italy	162
Austria	153
Switzerland	151
Norway	150
Denmark	142
Iceland	128
France	123
Belgium	120
Sweden	118
Canada	112
Japan	112
Australia	112
Portugal	105
Netherlands	103
Finland	100
Germany	98
Spain	96
Ireland	83
Korea	77
Greece	74
Hungary	52
Czech Republic	50
Poland	48
Mexico	40
Slovak Republic	30

The US spends $165 to get a point on PISA math, about 60% more than the OECD average

Average 104

The United States spends more than any other country per point on PISA mathematics test

Source: OECD 2006; Mckinsey analysis

The report further states that:

By underutilizing such a large proportion of the country's human potential, the US economy is less rich in skills than it could be.

The result is that American workers are, on average, less able to develop, master, and adapt to new productivity-enhancing technologies and methods than they could otherwise have been. Also, these achievement gaps have a clustering effect akin to economic dead zones, where communities with low-achieving local schools produce clusters of Americans largely unable to participate in the greater American economy due to a concentration of low skills, high unemployment, or high incarceration rates.

The McKinsey report does provide a reason for optimism inasmuch as America's history suggests that eventually we will be able to provide solutions to the problems of inequality and inequity, but to do so will take some hard work and vocal leaders. Put simply: how do we really make education work for all?

Notes

1. *A Nation at Risk: The Imperative for Educational Reform*, National Commission on Excellence in Education, last modified October 7, 1999, http://www2.ed.gov/pubs/NatAtRisk/index.html.

2. *ED IN 08 Unveils New Analysis and Report Card Surrounding 25th Anniversary of a Nation at Risk*, Strong American Schools Online Archive, accessed December 29, 2015, https://web.archive.org/web/20080828192156/http://www.edin08.com/uploadedFiles/Issues/A%20Stagnant%20Nation.pdf.

3. "'Nation at Risk': The Best Thing or the Worst Thing for Education?,"*USA Today Online*, updated August 1, 2008, http://usatoday30.usatoday.com/news/education/2008-04-22-nation-at-risk_N.htm.

4. Richard D. Kahlenberg, *Tough Liberal: Albert Shanker and the Battles Over Schools, Unions, Race, and Democracy* (New York: Columbia University Press, 2007), 5.

5. Diane Ravitch, *The Test of Time*, EducationNext Online, Spring 2003, vol. 3, no. 2, http://educationnext.org/thetestoftime/.

6. "'Nation at Risk': The Best Thing or the Worst Thing for Education?,"*USA Today Online*, updated August 1, 2008, http://usatoday30.usatoday.com/news/education/2008-04-22-nation-at-risk_N.htm.

7. *Overview and Inventory of State Requirements for School Coursework and Attendance*, Research and Development Report, June 1992, National Center for Education Statistics, http://nces.ed.gov/pubs92/92663.pdf.

8. *Budget History Tables, Education Department Budget History Table: FY 1980—FY 2016 President's Budget*, U.S. Department of Education Online, accessed December 29, 2015, http://www2.ed.gov/about/overview/budget/history/index.html.

9. *Progress Is No Accident: Why ESEA Can't Backtrack on High School Graduation Rates*, Alliance for Excellent Education, accessed December 29, 2015, http://all4ed.org/wp-content/uploads/2015/11/NoAccident.pdf.

10. Motoko Rich, *As Graduation Rates Rise, Experts Fear Diplomas Come Up Short*, New York Times Online, December 26, 2015, http://www.nytimes.com/2015/12/27/us/as-graduation-rates-rise-experts-fear-standards-have-fallen.html?_r=0.

11.   Dylan Scott, *48 percent of U.S. Schools Failed Federal Benchmarks*, Governing: The States and Localities, December 15, 2011, http://www.governing.com/news/local/gov-report-almost-half-US-schools-missed-AYP-2011.html.

12.   Christopher Ingraham, "Charting the Shocking Rise of Racial Disparity in Our Criminal Justice System,"*the Washington Post Online*, July 15, 2014, https://www.washingtonpost.com/news/wonk/wp/2014/07/15/charting-the-shocking-rise-of-racial-disparity-in-our-criminal-justice-system/.

13.   *The Economic Impact of the Achievement Gap in America's Schools*, McKinsey & Company: Social Sector Office, April 2009,http://mckinseyonsociety.com/downloads/reports/Education/achievement_gap_report.pdf.

4

Equal Opportunity Education: A Civil Rights Issue

As you've seen in some examples earlier and will see more prevalently moving forward throughout this book, much of the lack of access to education falls on those living in poverty, many of whom are black or Latino. And since so much of our current gridlock on education has its history rooted in the racial tensions of our country's past, I would be remiss if I did not share some of this history from my perspective: that of a boy growing up in the 1960s and 1970s coming to grips with America's racial and educational disparities.

A Family History of Activism

The combination of my parents and the confidence instilled in me by my first grade teacher, Helen Shelton, stoked a curiosity for learning in me at a young age that never diminished. Of course, it helped that my parents, particularly my father, continued to foster my learning. He was big on reading and always pressed us to read a lot, even while we were very young. He would tell us repeatedly how important it was for all of us, particularly as African Americans, to be literate. "Boy," he would say, "if you read, write and count, you can compete!" Still, however, we had to understand the complexities of competing in a world which wasn't always fair. And during the 1960s and 1970s, the time of my youth, our entire nation was in the midst of major social upheavals.

One day, when I was ten years old, the realities of the 1960s met squarely with my father's belief in personal learning and growth. My father and I were watching the evening news, when the grainy image of an elderly black man emerged on the screen. He had been walking home from church when several white men attacked him suddenly and brutally. They beat him with bats and kicked, punched, and taunted him. The old man had tried to get up, to keep walking, following every blow that knocked him to the ground. Despite his resolve, he was beaten to a bloody, unconscious pulp. I do not remember the name of the newscaster, but I will never forget the images.

What I saw changed my world. It was 1966. The images had come from Selma, Alabama. The country was in the middle of a social upheaval. My ten-year-old mind struggles to grasp the barbarism: Why were the men beating the old, defenseless man? Why wasn't he fighting back? How could the police let this happen?

Although I was aware of the civil rights problem in America, following that newscast I felt rage for the first time in my life. I could not understand why every black person, including my father, wasn't in the streets fighting for freedom.

"Daddy, let's find some white people to beat up." My logic was fast and furious—that of a ten-year-old boy. My father raised his head with a deep frown. He looked at me somberly for a few moments without saying a word. Fidgeting, I was afraid to say anything because he looked so serious—almost angry. When he finally spoke, he told me that before I ever act in response to something, I must completely understand every aspect of the problem and what caused it. "If, after you have completely grasped the problem, you still choose to fight, then so be it. But first you need to understand why you are fighting."

He then continued. "There is a book written about everything you face in life . . . when you face a problem, you should read about it, find out about it, then you can act." My father then reached for his bookshelf and gave me several books: *The Autobiography of Malcolm X*, Franz Fanon's *The Wretched of the Earth*, and *The Narrative of the Life of Frederick Douglass: An American Slave*.

This exchange with my father helped me appreciate the need to fully understand the depths of a problem before lashing out viscerally. Over the next few years, I read the books my father gave me along with many others. And he would sit down with me and talk about them. By reading all of the books he offered relating to racism, I gained various perspectives that I would not have seen otherwise, and furthermore, I developed a thirst for knowledge that could only be quenched through more reading, more learning, and more education.

Just before my twelfth birthday, Bobby Kennedy was running for president and his campaign was energizing significant parts of America. When it was announced that he would be making a campaign appearance in Indianapolis, my mother told my father she was taking all of us children to the rally. While my father was more analytical about the movement, my mother was a true activist. She was active with the local NAACP and the League of Women Voters. And she always took her children with her. A few years earlier, Alabama Governor George Wallace came to Indianapolis to speak at Butler University, right near our house. My mom and about twenty other women were there to protest. She gave me a sign to hold and when Governor Wallace got out of his town car, I broke through the barricade and shoved the sign in his face. The police threw me to the ground, and all those ladies started to hit the police. That was my mom. Years later when my parents came to visit me while I was in law school in DC, we saw a group of marchers near the Washington Monument. My mother said, "This is great. There is a march going on. Let's join it!" My father looked at me and shook his head. "Bettie Jane," he said, "do you even know who they are and why they are marching?" She just smiled and said, "It doesn't matter! We should still join them." We all just laughed.

When my mom said she was taking us to see Bobby Kennedy, it was no surprise to any of us. Little did we know how significant that night would be for America. Kennedy was speaking at Broadway Park (now King Park), located in a black, working-class neighborhood on the near east side of Indianapolis. My mom got us there early and we were right up front. In fact, when Kennedy did arrive, he walked right past us. I reached out and grabbed his wrist. I remember being a little mortified by how hairy he was. Other children and teens grabbed his hair. There was virtually no meaningful security between him and the crowd—surprising since his brother, President John Kennedy, had been killed just a few years earlier.

It started to get dark, and a light, misty rain began to fall. Kennedy and a few of his aides were standing on the back of a flat bed truck. We were all fired up waiting for him to speak. Then, there just seemed to be tension. Some of his team seemed to be arguing, others looked to be crying. I remember looking at Kennedy and thinking that he looked sick. After much obvious debate (we later learned that some of his aides and even Indianapolis Mayor Richard Lugar didn't want him to speak), Kennedy took the microphone and gave that now famous speech in which he announced that Martin Luther King had just been killed in Memphis. When he made the announcement, my mother, like everyone in the crowd, started to cry. I didn't cry, but I recall that the light rain made it look like I was crying as was everyone else. For some reason, I didn't want to look like I was crying. I felt I needed to be strong.

Kennedy then gave one of the most memorable, impromptu speeches in American political history. He talked about how easy it is to want to lash out at a time like this, how easy it is to hate. Quoting the poet *Aeschylus*, he said,

> Even in our sleep, pain which cannot forget
> falls drop by drop upon the heart,
> until, in our own despair,
> against our will,
> comes wisdom
> through the awful grace of God.

But the most powerful moment of that speech was when he informed the crowd that the early reports coming from Memphis seemed to indicate that a white man had killed Dr. King; that he knew how we all felt; he understood because a white man killed his brother.

Then he said, "what we need in the United States is not division; what we need in the United States is not hatred; what we need in the United States is not violence and lawlessness, but is love, and wisdom, and compassion toward one another, and a feeling of justice toward those who still suffer within our country, whether they be white or whether they be black."[1]

You could hear a pin drop on that misty, rainy night in that Indianapolis park while he was speaking.

The Indianapolis television stations played his speech all night over and over. When my father got home from the drug store, he and I sat and watched it, along with the television images of the riots taking place all over the country. Nearly every major city in America burned that night because they killed Dr. Martin Luther King, Jr. But not Indianapolis. Thanks to Bobby Kennedy.

Experiencing Racism Firsthand

Just as my father told me to think before I act back when I was young and hotheaded, he also warned me how to behave as a young black man after I received my driver's license and was given more freedom, from my family, that is. His reminders that I maintain a passive approach if I was ever pulled over by a white policeman served me well as a young man.

At Brebeuf Preparatory School I became a basketball star, was the first African American elected to a class office (junior class vice president), and was active in Junior Achievement. During my junior and senior years, I left home around 7 AM and after school, basketball practice, working at the drug store, and volunteer work, I wouldn't make it back until after nine at night. But I loved it. It was then that I realized how much of a "cause" guy I was. I possessed my father's need for analytical understanding and my mother's passion to fight against injustice. I was determined to go to law school and had dreams of being a civil rights lawyer.

As much as I loved Indiana, back then it was still a racist state. I faced innumerable racial incidents, but a few really stand out. Each incident centered around me being a basketball player at Brebeuf. Following the death of Dr. King and the riots that followed, many major American cities instituted curfews for youth under the age of eighteen. In effect, curfew laws mandated that no youth under eighteen could be on the streets after 11 PM, without being accompanied by a parent, guardian, or older relative. Some cities, like Indianapolis, made an exception for students participating in school-sponsored events. Brebeuf was located in the far north section of the city, and I lived closer to the inner city. So, quite naturally, I was regularly driving to and from my high school to participate in my team's basketball games. I had been more than prepped by my father as to how to handle being stopped by the police. He even went through a little role-playing for me. My younger brother, Edwin, used to watch us with his eyes open really wide. Dad made sure we understood to pull the car immediately to the shoulder as soon as we saw the police lights. We didn't want to give any indication of possible flight. Once the car was stopped, we were instructed to stay in the car, with both hands holding the top of the steering wheel. Very important. Both hands had to be visible at all times. Then, when the officer began his questions, we were instructed to answer in a calm clear voice, with "sir" at the end of each answer. Finally, we were told to never, ever show attitude or anger, no matter how much we were pushed. Thank God for my father. At age sixteen, I got my drivers' license. During my junior year, I was driving to the school for all of my games. With every away game we had, the bus generally got us back to the school after 11 PM. The first time I was stopped by the police was after the second or third game of the season. Driving south on Michigan Road near 86th Street, less than a mile from my high school, I was pulled over by a white police officer. I followed my father's directions exactly as I had been instructed. The officer came to the driver's window and did not waste any time in trying to taunt me. "What you doing up in this neighborhood, boy? Ain't many niggers up here. You done stole something?"

My head couldn't believe what my ears had heard. I was too shocked to be scared, but even now, I can feel what I felt that day.

"No sir," I said. "I am a student at Brebeuf High School and I am on the basketball team. The school bus just got back to the school and I am driving home."

"Boy, don't you know there is a curfew? I could lock you up right now. Hey, you got drugs in that gym bag? I think I smell marijuana!"

"No, sir. I do not do drugs. I am just going home."

"Get out of the car, boy. I need to search your car!"

Whereupon, I got out of my car and the officer searched it from front to back. I stood silently with my hands in full view (which is hard for me because I like having my hands in my pocket). After about ten minutes, he looked at me and said, "Get your ass home, boy!" And I left.

Dad and I debriefed over the incident and after telling me that I did good, he warned me that it would probably happen again. Boy, what an understatement. For the next two years—my junior and senior years—I was stopped approximately ten times by the same officer and his colleagues. I did everything to try to avoid them.

Instead of driving south on Michigan Road, I would try Ditch Road, then Meridian; soon it became a little game. The officers increasingly tried to bait me. They yelled in my face and threatened to plant drugs. During my senior year, when I started to excel on the basketball court, they began to taunt me about specific games. "You ain't as good as you think, boy."

Through it all, I kept my cool. Also, I purposely did not tell my dad about all of the stops. At one point, he talked about going to the officers' superiors, but I kept insisting I could handle it. Which I did. But it sure wasn't any fun.

During my junior year, there were six African-American players on my high-school basketball team. One Friday night we drove a couple of hours to play Yorktown High School, just outside of Muncie, Indiana. Muncie was known to be a popular place for the Ku Klux Klan some years earlier. After turning off the main road, we had to drive down a secondary road for about a mile before getting to the high-school gym. Our team was in a pretty jovial mood. We didn't have any racial incidents on our team; we all liked each other and got along great. I distinctly remember that someone was clowning around and we were all laughing. Our coach was trying to get us to quiet down. "You guys better get serious. We have to start concentrating on this game!" But even as he was admonishing us, he was smiling. We were having a good time.

As we got closer to the gym, we noticed a fire. At first, we thought the gym was on fire, because the flames were close to the gymnasium. The closer we got, the more unmistakable the source of the fire. Burning crosses!

In an instant, all of the laughter died down. Everyone, including coach Lee, grew deathly silent. As the bus driver slowed down, I started to count the crosses. At first, I could only count five. I tried to lighten the mood, by saying to my friend and fellow African-American teammate Paul Hines, "Hey, Paul. There are only five crosses. They missed me. I am ok." No one laughed or even smiled. Paul just pointed toward one of the crosses up front which was obscuring another cross. "There you are over there, Kevin. They didn't miss you."

No one mentioned the incident during the game or on the way back. During his pregame talk, all Coach said was, "Guys, you are here to play basketball. There is no need to worry about anything else." But, while running from the locker room to the basketball court, many of us did begin to worry. As we were about to jog onto the court, we had to pass Yorktown's pom-pom girls, which also included three or four junior pom-pom girls who were about seven or eight years old. As each one of the African-American players ran past one of the young junior pom-pom girls, she would wave her pom-pom at us while counting "Nigger number 1, nigger number 2," and so on. We lost the game and there was no clowning or laughing on the way back to Indianapolis.

Following Brebeuf, I attended Wabash College in Crawfordsville, Indiana. Wabash is also all-male and is known for its academic rigor and its ability to build future leaders. I thoroughly enjoyed the intellectual discourses in my political science classes. I gained a better understanding of democracy, of governing, and of American politics. I had a stellar basketball career, and I was also chairman of the Malcolm X Institute for Black Studies. As much as I enjoyed Wabash on many levels, I still had to deal with racism. Unlike high school, however, the problem was on my team. Early into my sophomore season, I was about to break into the starting lineup as a shooting guard. Frankly, I had expected to be starting as a freshman, but our coach had allegiances to the five starters, all seniors, all white, and all starters since they were freshman. Those guys also happened to be members of the same fraternity. As my sophomore year began, it was obvious that the starters were especially threatened by me and another African-American player, Bob Knowling, who was a junior. What made matters worse was that each of the starters' parents came to all of the games, sat right behind our bench, and even traveled with the team to all of our away games. Right before one of our home games, the coach told me that I would be starting. He really didn't have much of a choice. I was the best guard on the team, and we lost our first couple of games with the players he had been playing. And even though I was the sixth man instead of a starter in those first couple of games, it was evident that the team played best when I entered the game. We played even better when Bob (who was the backup point guard) and I were playing at the same time.

I was excited to be starting, especially in front of our home crowd. Some teammates offered encouragement, though the gang of five didn't say a word to me. Then I received the shock of my life when my name was announced as one of the starters. Folks from our home crowd, most notably the bleacher section that contained my teammates' fraternity brothers, started booing loudly. Then some started to call me nigger. I looked at Bob and the other two African Americans on the team with obvious disbelief. Bob said, "That's alright, Blood, I got your back." As I was running onto the court, it hit me that the parents in the back of our bench were booing as well. Welcome to the starting lineup!

It pretty much went that way the rest of the season. I was in and out of the lineup, not because of the quality of my play—I was still the best guard on the team—but because of the pressure the coach got from those players and their parents. The coach had no control at all over the team. And it was rough. I remember wondering how these adults could hate me so much just because of the color of my skin, especially since we were on the same team! For me, Bob, and the other two African Americans on the team, Brandon Johnson and Joe Mims, we were the only ones we had. I kept thinking, "they are trying to break me." But it would never happen. I knew that I came from good stock.

The most trying part of the season occurred during the holidays as we played our west coast schedule. Those racist parents accompanied the team for the entire trip. They ate with us, rode on the bus with us, and even sat through some of our practices—something unheard of on most teams. Whenever Bob and I were in the game, the parents would curse at us from behind our bench. They would also call us nigger. During one of those games, while I was on the court, one of the parents stood up and yelled at me, "Pass the ball you stupid nigger!" Next thing I know, Bob had turned around and gone into the stands after that parent. Other players broke up the scuffle, but at least they stopped using the word nigger after that.

I did, however, get the last laugh. A new coach, Mac Petty, took over the team after my sophomore year. He was a good guy and did not tolerate the racial mess. As a result, I was allowed to concentrate on playing ball and I flourished. My teammates voted me the most valuable player during both my junior and senior years, the first African American in school history to accomplish such a feat. I was also chosen as an NCAA District All American. Through my basketball success, I was able to start a basketball camp for grade-school children. As a result, I developed lifelong friendships with local residents I would not have met otherwise. All of these residents were white, and they all are terrific human beings. They supported me throughout my time at Wabash and remain friends with me to this day. Because of our bond of brotherhood that steeled us during those difficult days, Bob Knowling will always be one of my dearest friends. He has also become a successful business CEO. Not long ago, with no bitterness or regret, he donated millions of dollars to the college for a new gymnasium. I can only imagine what the gang of five thinks about the Wabash College basketball games being played in *Knowling Field House.*

By the time I entered Howard Law, I had already experienced a rich, challenging academic schooling which was further nurtured by supportive parents. Yes, I had some racial issues I had to deal with, but they paled in comparison to the depth and breadth of my highly positive upbringing. It wasn't until I was taking classes at Howard that I realized how lucky I was, and how stark the contrast was between my educational experience and those experienced by many of my classmates. Howard itself presented a contrast among its student body. Howard University is considered the elite among the historically black universities in America, and its alumni roster is a who's who list of successful and accomplished African Americans. At the height of segregation, schools like Howard were the only places from which blacks could receive graduate degrees. As recently as the 1990s, 50 percent of all African-American doctors and lawyers graduated from historically black universities like Howard.[2] As a result, Howard's law school in particular had students who could get into nearly any school they wanted, but Howard was their first choice, but also students for whom Howard was their only choice. Similarly, some students had legacy ties to Howard and came from the black elite, while others were the first in their family to matriculate past high school—all of which made for a diverse and interesting environment. In getting to know my classmates and some of their stories, I was struck by the educational disparities in America. Many of my classmates from the south attended "schools" that were just one step above the one-room schoolhouse my father attended in Aiken, South Carolina, in the 1940s. Still others had to navigate through gangs and burned-out teachers in cities like New York, Chicago, and Detroit.

Experiencing racism firsthand in childhood and young adulthood and growing to see the importance of education on improving communities, both later influenced my decision to run for public office. These were the issues I knew I cared about, so I just had to stand up for what I believed in and work to make a difference.

Notes

1. For a video of the speech, see "The Greatest Speech Ever—Robert F Kennedy Announcing the Death of Martin Luther King," posted by Mohammad Azzam on January 4, 2013, https://www.youtube.com/watch?v=GoKzCff8Zbs. For a transcript of the speech, please see "Robert F. Kennedy: Remarks on the Assassination of Martin Luther King, Jr.," American Rhetoric, Top 100 Speeches, accessed December 29, 2015, http://www.americanrhetoric.com/speeches/rfkonmlkdeath.html.

2. Nikole Hannah-Jones, "A Prescription for More Black Doctors," *The New York Times* Online, September 9, 2015, http://www.nytimes.com/2015/09/13/magazine/a-prescription-for-more-black-doctors.html.

5

Public Service in Our Nation's Capital

In 1981, two years before *A Nation at Risk* was released, I gradu-ated from the Howard University School of Law in Washington, DC, the same law school that produced Thurgood Marshall. As the graduating class president, I gave the commencement address. I was super proud to be a Howard alum. Law school had been a natural extension of my learning and growth process. Like my dad always told us, "grade school, high school, college and beyond." Getting my law degree didn't make me feel extraordinarily special. I was doing what I was supposed to do. Unlike many, I was blessed to have received a great educational experience. And I still wanted to change the world; I just wasn't exactly sure how. For many years growing up in Indianapolis in the midst of the social changes I mentioned above, I had dreams of being a civil rights lawyer in the tradition of Thurgood Marshall. Indeed, that was what, in part, drove me to enroll at Howard University. While in law school, I still enjoyed the thought of being a litigator, but my interest drifted away from civil rights law. I had really good courtroom skills and decided to hone that craft. For most of the 1980s I was having great success trying cases in the DC courts, both local and federal. Before long, I was itching to get involved in the community and decided that the best way to make a difference was to run for public office. By 1992, I was firmly entrenched in the local DC community and I formally entered the DC political arena.

On the night I upset longtime DC councilmember H.R. Crawford in the Democratic primary, which virtually assured that I would be the next councilmember from Ward 7 in the nation's capital, I was on top of the world. Once it was clear that I had won the election, a who's who of local Washington came to my victory celebration.

Several members of Congress also dropped by. Television cameras from all of the local channels were front and center. Local reporters from the major newspapers were all clamoring for interviews. I was the new flavor of the month.

While I was waiting for all of the cameras to get set up, I noticed that my father was watching all of the goings-on with great interest. I could see that he was proud, but it was clear that he was somewhat unnerved by all of the attention being directed toward his oldest child. He walked up to me, elbowed his way through some of the back patters, and said, "Son, let's go back to your office and talk for a minute. It won't take long."

I said, "Sure, dad!"

I then excused myself from the gathering throng and escorted my father to my private campaign office, away from the crowd. After I closed the door behind me, both I and my father sat in chairs that directly faced each other.

As was his style, he didn't waste any time with small talk.

"Son," he began, "you have always been a good boy and you have a good heart. You have always made me and your mom proud."

I smiled and tried to cut him off.

"Thanks, dad!" I said. "I am on my way . . ."

It was then his turn to cut me off.

"Let me finish, son. I am very proud of you despite becoming a lawyer and now, a politician." We both laughed. Our private little joke. My dad, like my two sisters and my brother, had a bent toward math and science. In fact, my brother Edwin won the Indiana state science fair when he was in sixth grade. My dad would have rather seen me go to medical school. I used to jokingly tell him that since I could talk, I needed to play to my strength. He then continued.

"Seriously, son, I am proud of you and I know you are doing this because you want to make a difference. I truly believe that. You have always been that kind of kid. But you need to know this." (He then pointed out toward the main room where the crowd was waiting.) "Ten years from now, if all those people are still cheering for you, you have wasted your time. If you look at history, no one who has done anything to help their fellow man, no one who has really made a difference was being cheered while they were doing it. Think about it. Martin Luther King, Abraham Lincoln, George

Washington, even Jesus Christ. They all caught hell while they were trying to help others. Now, later they were celebrated. But for most, that happens after they are dead. So, boy, you will know when you are doing something meaningful in this job when they aren't cheering for you; when they are giving you a hard time and all you have to fall back on are your principles and what you believe."

He then hugged me and we both left the room so I could give my speech and begin my public life in earnest. Little did I know how much my father's words would serve to fortify me when I decided to challenge the education status quo later on as the chair of the education committee.

In 1993, when I was sworn into office as the new DC councilmember representing Ward 7, I was hoping to make a difference in my southeast DC neighborhood which, at the time, was beset with problems of crime, drugs, and violence. Education was not my focus when I entered office. Like many people, I thought that education was a school board's issue.

When I arrived, my ward was in dire need of a fresh approach. Ward 7 comprises parts of far northeast and southeast DC bordering Maryland. It has some terrific middle-class neighborhoods, but also had some of the toughest, crime-ridden areas in the city. Many believed that the ten public housing projects in the ward were a big source of the problem. While there was some truth to that, I came to believe that the biggest problem was the quality of the schools. During my first few years, I aggressively did all the things a big city ward councilmember was expected to do: hosted Christmas parties, gave away Thanksgiving turkeys, visited senior centers, patrolled with the police, met with pastors and other ward leaders, attended wakes and funerals, went to various community meetings, hosted town hall meetings, did neighborhood cleanups, organized a Ward 7 day parade, and even sponsored my own basketball league for children. I also had to deal with weekly crises like the headline-making drive-by shooting, the widespread fire at a public housing complex, the service station gas leak, and the hostage-taking incident. (I would get nervous when the television stations would say: breaking news!) Oh, and of course, snowstorms. One fun highlight occurred when, in cahoots with a friendly police officer, we commandeered a city snowplow and started to plow selected streets. I loved the look on a couple of my political opponents' faces when they saw me leading a snow truck down their block: priceless. All the while, I was learning about my ward, its people, its challenges and opportunities.

When I first entered office, I believed that economic opportunity was the key to solving the problems of my ward or, for that fact, any urban city. I just didn't grasp the importance of education. That all changed after I spent more time in my ward and began to connect the dots.

My understanding of the connection between education and opportunity first occurred during my visits to Lorton Penitentiary, our local prison. It was during one of those visits that I was told that 85 percent of the inmate population was high-school dropouts. I was floored by that. I had no idea that the vast majority of our prison population had dropped out of school. I had been very active working to curb crime in my ward. The crack epidemic had hit my ward hard. Along the way, I ended up getting to know a few young guys who were selling on the street. Having been apprised of the prison/school dropout statistic, I began to ask some of these guys about their education. Then I asked another. And another. I talked to my friend and mentor, Ike Fulwood, a former DC police chief. Ike grew up in DC and knew the streets well. Once he retired, he dedicated his time to help turn around young guys who were lost. Years later, he and I would start a mentoring program for boys, which was very successful. Ike told me that he believed that these guys dropped out of school because they felt that school had nothing for them. As one young man told me, "Councilman, I was never celebrated in school. They made me feel like a nobody. At least on the streets, I am somebody." There is no doubt in my mind that a good number of these men's lives would have been far different if they were in schools that met their needs.

Further instances that showed me the importance of education began to pop up. Soon after visiting Lorton, I began to work with Safeway officials and folks from the then Housing and Urban Development Secretary Andrew Cuomo's office to get a new Safeway in my ward. We hadn't had a new grocery store in years, so this was a big deal. Like any ward representative, I was hammering Safeway about committing to hire not just DC residents, but Ward 7 residents specifically. One Safeway official suggested that I work on getting our schools right. "We need people with basic reading and math skills," he said. "It would help if you put more pressure on your schools to get better."

Once, while visiting a drug treatment facility, I asked the director about the educational attainment of those she treats. She matter-of-factly said that most of them hadn't finished high school.

Slowly but surely, the light bulb was turning on. I was beginning to make the practical connection between education and strong communities. And I wasn't learning it in a book or from a lecture. I was living it while representing my constituents.

I soon started to ask more detailed questions of principals and teachers during my school visits. While many were doing extraordinary work, many others weren't serving our children well at all. I remember one highly regarded teacher told me, "Councilman, we do the best we can, but there is only so much you can do to help these ghetto children." I was thunderstruck, but really didn't know how to respond. I realized that education was indeed the key, but I didn't know how I could create lasting change that could help these children whose future success seemed out of my control as a councilmember. Furthermore, as much as I wanted to help the situation, I struggled with whether it was my place; wasn't this the job of the school board? Well yeah, it was, but I soon came to find that they were also part of the problem. Like many other school boards around the country, they really didn't oversee policy and were immersed in micro-managing and deal-making.

As I was nearing the end of my first term and itching to find a way to get more engaged with school issues, a conversation with councilmember Bill Lightfoot gave me clarity about how to focus my future public service. Bill was retiring from the council, and over coffee he told me that his one major regret was that he never sought the chairmanship of the education committee. "We spend all of our time preventing disasters in our wards—whether it is a fiscal crisis or a crime spree. We are always putting out fires and thinking that issues like education are a luxury. What we never stopped to consider was the connection between lack of opportunities and access to education, and what was playing out on the streets—that perhaps education is the root of our problem. If I were you, Kevin, I would take over the education committee. Then, you can make a difference."

It was a catalytic moment for me. I had really never thought about taking over the education committee. The committee was chaired by a former teacher and school board member who had fought the battle for education for years and had served the city well. Then in her eighties, she unfortunately did not have the energy to take on the dramatic reforms that were needed at the time, and schools were receiving little, if any, oversight.

One of Bill's final initiatives was helping councilmember Frank Smith shepherd through the DC Charter School bill. Without knowing much about charter schools at all, I voted for the bill because I intuitively believed that we needed to try different approaches. Now, Bill was suggesting that I take over the committee that would set and oversee the budget for our entire education, library, and recreation systems.

I began to ask my supporters and friends what they thought about me taking over the education committee. Few, if any, were supportive. "It will kill you politically," I would hear. Or, "It's a black hole that can't be fixed. Leave it to the school board." The more people I talked with, the more convinced I was that I should fight to take over the committee. It became clear that part of the reason why our schools were a mess is that our best and brightest were avoiding the challenge while our school board members were looking to elevate to the council. Bill was right. In order to really make a difference, I needed to step up and channel my efforts toward education. And that's what I did. I became the chair of the education committee in 1997 and held the position until I left office eight years later in 2005. Looking back, I can say that in public service, I truly found my life's work.

6

Heading Up the Education Committee

In late 1996, when I took over the DC Council's education committee, not only were we about to welcome a new DC public schools superintendent, but the council had also just passed charter school legislation. As the new point person overseeing education in DC, I was tasked with overseeing both approaches.

When I became the chair of the education committee, things were in rough shape. Under the previous chair's leadership, the schools had pretty much been receiving a blank check. There was virtually no accountability for the dollars spent and the results were embarrassing. While many parents were frustrated, most low-income African-American parents didn't know what they didn't know. They were used to their neighborhood school which was probably the same school their parents and grandparents attended. They had no idea how far many of these schools had fallen in terms of the quality of teaching.

For the next few years, I was deeply immersed in both the reform of DC public schools and growing our new charter school movement. Beyond navigating between parents, the DC public school system, community leaders, and my colleagues, I put a lot of my focus and attention toward the development of charter schools. It didn't take long to see how much of a cesspool existed in the school system and that meaningful, substantive change would take years at best. For parents in my ward, however, they didn't have the luxury of waiting and so I wanted to act fast. Needless to say, my staunch advocacy for charter schools was not received well by everyone. More and more, the teachers union was starting to give me a hard time about my support of charter schools, even while I was giving teachers and the DC public school system more money. Indeed, my early support for charter schools was the main reason why the teachers union came out so strongly against me when I ran for mayor the next year in 1998.

Still, I found my greatest base of support among parents with children enrolled in school. I spent a lot of time talking with them and encouraging them to testify at my hearings. I also went to great lengths to help populate the boards of those starting charter schools with trusted community members. That effort alone helped to ease the tension associated with "outsiders coming into our neighborhoods to educate our children." At the time, I didn't know much about education reform or the charter school movement. I was involved in the daily grind of trying to push our system and those around it to do better for our children. And I was developing a sense of urgency around my expectations for better schools.

Some of the parents from schools that needed the most change were the most resistant to change, even many of the parents whose children attended underperforming schools in my ward. Keep in mind that many of these parents—and even their parents—attended these schools when they worked well. Nostalgia and sentimentality often meant more than test scores. On the other hand, many white parents—most notably from west of Rock Creek Park and the Capitol Hill area—were trying to make sure that their safe haven of schools was preserved. As is the case in most major cities, even today, wealthy white families are able to leverage their influence to develop and maintain quality teachers and principals in their neighborhood public schools. In DC even when the DC public schools facilities management was a mess, those parents west of the park found ways to get the rules adjusted so they could financially support supplies, blackboards, and a host of other items that their school's principal needed. It didn't take long for a new DC superintendent to learn that keeping this constituency happy made his or her life a lot easier. The bottom line was that while most DC residents recognized the need for change in our school system, many felt that the change should take place at someone else's school but not theirs.

Once I began to look closely at the outputs in DC public schools, it became clear to me that change was needed at all levels, from the school board to the teachers' unions. Early on, the district had some great superintendents like Vincent Reed and Floretta McKenzie, who were excellent by all measures. Part of their success was their ability to maneuver through and rise above the politics of the board.

This system worked well during the late 1970s and early 1980s, but then the politics took hold and more board members came in with political aspirations. They would take actions such as steering contracts toward potential political allies and friends, who, for example, claimed to have a construction business but clearly knew nothing about patching roofs. Some board members cut deals with an incoming superintendent: you hire this principal and I will approve your appointment. And the deals continued once the new superintendent was in place. In the 1980s, you could look through the school system's list of employees and find scores of employees with the same surnames as board members: a custodian here, a teacher there, an administrator elsewhere.

Then, there was the teachers union. After I took over the education committee, then union president Barbara Bullock came into my office with several of her lieutenants letting me know that they thought I had potential before I voted for the charter school bill. She further said that since I chair the committee, I don't have to fund charters, and that they would be watching. Thank you very much. Over the next several years, the union would continue to give me a hard time, particularly when I ran for mayor in 1998. As fate would have it, however, Bullock and a couple of her deputies ended up in jail for diverting over six million dollars' worth of teachers union dues to themselves for their personal use. These factors and others eventually led to the complete and utter destruction of the DC public school system.

The final blow to the DC public school system occurred in 1994, right after DC residents returned Marion Barry to the mayor's office, when it was discovered that DC had a $500 million dollar deficit. Congress was clearly not happy and thus established a federally appointed control board to oversee the city's finances and theoretically work on reform. Under the new arrangement, the mayor would still technically run the city government, but the five federally appointed control board members would have to approve all city expenditures. Practically speaking, once you control the money, you run the show. So the new control board ran the city.

47

One of the control board's first orders of business was an intense review of the public schools. Among other findings, the evaluation noted that cronyism engulfed the system, test scores were among the lowest in the country, the facilities were in shambles, and the children were not learning. The control board stripped the elected board of its powers and appointed an emergency board of trustees to run the schools.

The control board wanted to show it was serious about making a difference, and that is why it focused on schools. Along with the city's deficit, the schools were the most obvious examples of the district's failures. At one point, it seemed that every week brought a new story highlighting the schools' fiascos. One such debacle was the Service Master contract, a multimillion dollar contract for the maintenance of schools, which had been steered to a school board member's friend—with disastrous results. The front page of the *Washington Post* highlighted in embarrassing detail what the city was paying for maintenance and how that maintenance was not being done.[1] Later, the city was overwhelmed with constant stories about leaking roofs and dilapidated classrooms.[2]

With parents, schools, and advocacy groups uniting to sue the school system over inadequate facilities, the control board made a strategic decision to show it was serious about reform. It appointed a retired African-American general, Julius Becton, to run the schools. He, in turn, brought in the US Army Corps of Engineers to handle all school repairs and maintenance.

Against this backdrop, I officially took over the education committee in January 1997, right after General Becton was appointed superintendent. We were all getting used to having the control board as overseers, and I was also trying to keep them and Superintendent Becton grounded. My frustration with the control board stemmed from their insistence on reform taking place from the top down. They didn't understand that being well intentioned, honorable, credentialed, and respected with status and stature alone means nothing when you are trying to reform public education. Public education reform can only happen when you involve the community that is supposed to benefit from your efforts. An entire community must be invested in children's schooling for it to be successful.

We also had to deal with integrating the charter school approach into our policy and budget-making process. Since the control board was used to having no public meetings and operating in secrecy, I took the opposite approach: I decided to shine a light on everything through public hearings. Those hearings became legendary. At the time, it was the only way for the public to participate in the reform of our education system. And the hearings were long and cumbersome. For example, my budget oversight hearing on DC public schools started at 10 AM and ended at 3 AM the next morning. I would have parents, teachers, community activists, school board members, students, any and all stakeholders participate. I also made sure that Superintendent Becton and control board member Connie Newman testified. Connie was the control board member on the point for education issues, and I always thought she was terrific. She understood the tension associated with the control board's role, so she did what she could to respect the elected officials and the public. I enjoyed working with her. Over time, even Superintendent Becton came to accept the public hearings. One thing was clear: if you know you may be asked in public about a decision or an action taken, you give more thought to the ramifications of that decision or action.

After a while, I began to understand how the entrenched school bureaucracy unwittingly works against children; far too many school district central office staff do little, if anything, during their work day to contribute to the learning needs of children. This was vividly demonstrated during one of my education committee oversight hearings. Superintendent Becton sat at the witness table with about three of his top staff members seated next to him. As was the case with all government witnesses, I had them all stand, raise their right hand, and swear to tell the truth. Sitting in the first three or four rows behind the general were approximately fifteen to twenty central office school system senior staffers. As I was listening to General Becton make his opening remarks, I started to focus on all of those staffers filling up the seats in the council chambers. I then started to think about a couple of recent school visits in southeast DC, in which virtually none of the children were learning. Yet, once again, there didn't seem to be any sense of urgency about the poor quality of these children's schools. Instead, the school system's top brass was sitting in the council's chambers ostensibly waiting to help their superintendent answer my questions. I wondered, "What do all of these central office workers do? Is there a connection between the work they do in offices downtown and the lack of learning taking place in some of our schools around the city? Have these senior staffers even thought about such a connection? Do they care?"

I let General Becton finish his statement and then began to ask him questions. Predictably, he started to turn around to get assistance from some of the staff seated in the audience. In an impromptu moment, I then started to speak to the staffers in the audience.

"I want all of the DC public school system employees in attendance to stand to be sworn in for testimony," I said.

Becton and his executive team were aghast. "What's the problem, Mr. Chairman?" the general asked me.

"I just want to ask a few of these folks what they do and how their day to day work helps grow the student achievement of our children. I know they are here to support you, but I would like to know what they do."

Becton didn't know what to say.

Using my gavel, I began to point at random staffers in the audience from the council dais.

"You, in the second row, please step forward and have a seat at the witness table. Sir, please give me your job title and walk me through a typical work day for you."

The staffer then said he was the assistant to the assistant deputy of some school system division and he told me about his typical day of meetings and office work.

I then asked the most important question.

"Sir, we have over half of the children in our schools not performing at grade level. In some of our schools, the vast majority of children can't read. So tell me, how does what you do every day help us help Johnny and Jane learn how to read? Or to count? Or to learn?"

Silence.

Finally, the witness hemmed and hawed about the importance of his job relative to the school system's central office operations that gives schools and teachers the support they need to do their jobs.

"O.K. But Johnny and Jane still can't read," I said.

And so it went. I only called up a couple more staffers to answer my questions, but the point was made. For far too many school systems' central office staffers—both in DC and around the country—there is really no connection between the work they do and the education we are (supposedly) providing to our children. From the dais that day, I hammered that point. It made no sense to me that our school system central staff was so disconnected from the folks on the ground. And it was not right. General Becton tried to stress how important each staffer was to the school system's mission, but even he could not explain to me how the staffers' jobs contributed to student achievement or children's learning.

At my next oversight hearing, General Becton was only accompanied by his three executive team members. Despite their intention to shirk the issue (or at least protect their reputation at hearings), these meetings became immensely instructive in getting to the bottom of why our schools were failing and what we could do to fix it.

Notes

1. Debbi Wilgoren, Valerie Strauss, and David A. Vise, "One Year Later, Becton Still Struggles," *The Washington Post*, Archives Online, November 18, 1997, http://www.washingtonpost.com/wp-srv/local/longterm/library/dc/schools/becton2.htm.

2. "Hearing, Before the Subcommittee on the District of Columbia of the Committee on Government Reform and Oversight House of Representatives One Hundred Fifth Congress Second Session," accessed on December 29, 2015, http://files.eric.ed.gov/fulltext/ED425615.pdf.

7

Running for Mayor and Growing Charter Schools in DC

In 1998, I decided to run for mayor of the District of Columbia. Marion Barry was still the mayor, but it had become increasingly obvious that he was having a harder time with Congress and the business community than he did during his first tenure as mayor, when he was one of the best mayors in the country. He may have been able to get back in office after his scandal, but his ability to govern would never be the same. He rightly decided that he would not seek another term as mayor.

Two of my council colleagues were also vying for the post. I had considered them both as friends, but we all soon began to snipe at each other as we readied ourselves for the campaign. I was viewed as a favorite, but we all believed that a credible outsider would emerge as a challenger. With all that had happened in the city including Marion's election four years earlier, the city's financial collapse and the resulting federally appointed control board, there was a clear "throw the bums out" mindset in the city. Though I have strong appeal among African-American voters in the city, I was not as well known among white voters. I was also hampered by the fact that I represented the ward right next to Marion's ward—on that other side of town.

None of us anticipated the outsider challenge that we received. Anthony Williams was the CFO for the Clinton administration's Department of Agriculture when Marion Barry appointed him to be the CFO for the city. Under the control board legislation, the mayor still had the authority to choose the CFO for the city, but once appointed, that person had to report to the control board. Tony was a bow tie-wearing self-described bean-counting nerd, so I know when Marion appointed him, he never expected him to emerge as a political candidate for mayor, given the tension he stirred as CFO. Shortly after stepping into office, Tony made headlines for coldly firing a bunch of longtime city workers and having the police escort them out of their respective buildings. He then made several caustic comments about the city workforce. Local DC, unlike its federal city counterpart, prides itself on being touchy feely and the city expects the same from its leadership. Tony Williams was just the opposite. Yet after years of riding the Marion Barry roller coaster, DC residents were ready for someone who was the exact opposite of Marion.

As we got closer and closer to the election, it became clear that I was the only one who had a chance to beat Tony. Soon, Tony became the darling candidate of the *Washington Post* and upper-class white residents. As I expected, the teachers union also weighed in heavily. They ran television ads with a superimposed X running across my face. I had to explain to my then eight-year-old son Eric that I did, indeed, like his teacher.

As is the case with most hotly contested, high-profile campaigns, the tension between my camp and Tony's was extreme. It didn't help things when I didn't immediately concede election night. My staff kept insisting that I wait until all the votes were counted, but that is no real excuse. It made me look small. But, as a result, folks in Tony's campaign were worried that I might go rogue and support the popular Republican nominee, councilmember Carol Schwartz. A couple of days after the primary election, I got a call from my father in Indianapolis. He and my mother had come to DC for the final days of the campaign, but left soon thereafter. "Hi, son," my father said. "Guess who is sitting in our living room, about to join us for dinner?"

"Who?" I asked.

"That Tony Williams boy's mother. She just knocked on our door."

Needless to say, I was shocked. I saw Mrs. Williams quite a bit on the campaign trail and everyone knew she was a free spirit. Feisty to the core, she would sometimes break out into a song at campaign events. Tony would just roll his eyes. But she was no dummy. She took it upon herself to fly to Indianapolis to urge my parents to talk me into supporting her son. She kept maintaining that if Tony and I could find a way to work together, we could do good for the city and its children. Some woman.

A few days later, Tony and I held a joint press conference in which I enthusiastically endorsed him.

Around the time Tony took office, I had decided that I was going to redouble my efforts to improve education in the city and I poured myself into my committee work. By the year 2000, our charter schools were doing well and many had a lengthy waiting list. In addition, the control board statute was expiring soon and we had to decide who was going to run the schools. At the time, I had a young committee clerk working for me named Adrian Fenty. Adrian had been a field coordinator for my mayoral campaign and I was so impressed with him that I hired him on my staff. He and I worked feverishly on a proposal that would turn control of the schools over to the mayor. A couple of cities had tried it, and Adrian and I thought it would work perfectly in DC. The thing we didn't want to do was return the schools back under the control of the elected school board. I spoke with Tony at length about the idea and he agreed with us. Soon, both his staff and mine were working to make this happen. Unfortunately, this was the one time in which the mayor and I couldn't convince my colleagues to follow our lead. They were getting enormous pressure about continuing what Congress had started: the further dis-empowerment of an elected body of the District. After much political wrangling, we all agreed on a compromise hybrid board to pick the superintendent and oversee the schools. Of the nine members, five were to be elected and four were to be appointed by the mayor and confirmed by the council. We placed the proposal on a referendum to be voted in by the citizens and it passed.

Years later, Adrian Fenty would become DC's mayor, succeeding Tony Williams in 2006. After he appointed Michelle Rhee as chancellor of DC public schools, I thought about the original mayoral takeover proposal that Adrian and I worked on so intensely while he was on my staff. As mayor, Adrian lobbied the council hard to give him control over the schools. The legislation that the council eventually passed which gave him that power was virtually the same bill we had offered six years earlier, proving once again that timing is everything.

* * *

Being as focused as I was on the minutiae of education reform in DC, I was almost oblivious at first to education reform efforts taking place throughout America. After going through a period focused on reshaping schools and curricula, the 1990s brought a more dedicated focus to leadership. Every time a major city had a superintendent vacancy, the dance got started, similar to the way major sports teams court free agent stars and try to entice them to join their team. For each vacancy, several highly regarded names would apply. And most interviewed very well. Years later, when I was part of the team interviewing candidates vying to become the DC superintendent, I was pretty amazed at how well the major candidates did during the interview process. Like all educators, they were loaded with statistics and data that proved their competence. And for every weak data point, there was a strong explanation or rebuttal. The key buzzwords they all relied on were *time and money.* "I can get the reading scores up for your disadvantaged students, but I need the time and the resources," the typical candidate would say. Then they would show how they moved the needle upward for the disadvantaged children in the school district they are currently running, showing gains of, say, 3 to 4 percent over the last three years. But the district's school board reneged on the promise to fully fund the reform plan. "If you will commit the resources, I can make more dramatic gains," the candidate would say. It was during this period that the dumbing down began, and we started to lower our expectations, both of our children and the schools they attended. This is when the excuses became more prevalent. "We could get better outputs, if ___." Just fill in the blank. During superintendent interviews, you never heard candidates talk about changing the tenure rules or committing to dramatic results too quickly. Indeed, this is when the three- to five-year reform plan du jour became commonplace. Most of these candidates would lay out a plan that called for five years of commitment from the school district in exchange for certain modest academic gains. It was rare, however, for a superintendent in a major city to stay on the job for all of those five years. DC had approximately six superintendents in ten years prior to the current Chancellor Kaya Henderson. It is hard to maintain continuity under those circumstances.

In fairness, most superintendents are forced to lead systems that are wholly resistant to change with rules that are politically impossible to change, which is probably why during the early 2000s, many cities were aggressively looking for nontraditional superintendents who could think out of the box and had more of a sense of urgency to press for change.

That lack of urgency also added to the growing popularity of charter schools, especially in many urban areas. Charter schools are public schools that receive government funding but are free to offer innovative curriculum, special incentives for teachers, and targeted education to children. Charter schools are often created by local nonprofits, colleges and universities, state or local charter school boards, and local school boards. Ideally, charter schools have autonomy—meaning that they are free to create diverse and high-achieving educational environments without many of the bureaucratic requirements faced by traditional public schools. Most states have some form of law allowing for the creation of charter schools. The charter school concept was first conceived by college professor Ray Budde, who in the 1980s wrote a paper, *Education by Charter*, as an idea for redistricting school districts.[1] Minnesota passed the first charter school bill in 1991, and charter schools have grown every year since that time.[2] Although they have long been viewed as a conservative Republican-driven initiative, Bill Clinton was actually an early supporter of charter schools and made federal grants available for those wanting to start a charter school.[3] When I embraced charters on the eve of my education committee chairmanship, I had no idea how quickly they would come to be viewed as the primary public alternative to the traditional public school. As of 2013 there were over three million children attending charter schools in America, and charter schools are so popular that there are over one million students on charter schools waiting lists nationwide.[4] Parents love the innovation provided by many charter schools and welcome not having to deal with local school district bureaucracy. Of course, traditionalists associated with standard local school districts argue against the charter school concept because charter schools do not fall directly under local school district control. But that fact has apparently made them more popular with parents. For instance, various studies suggest that low-income disadvantaged students do better at charter schools than traditional public schools.[5]Additionally, all charter school laws allow for them to be closed if they do not serve children. So let's close the bad ones. In fact, I believe that we should shut down any school that is not working for children. Finally, when viewing the effectiveness of charter schools state by state, it is obvious that charter schools in any given state are only as good as the law that created them. Keep in mind that some charter laws are just plain bad, largely because they were passed as a politically compromised version that was vastly different from the original proposal: a common problem with the politics of education. Are charter schools the answer? It depends on the law in your state and it depends on individual parent's needs. Remember, educational choice is not a zero sum game in which one needs to pick sides. Rather, we need a wide range of quality options to offer parents so that they can find the best fit for their child. Here, we need to elevate the discussion. In reality, it is more about school fit than school choice. Each parent should have the luxury of picking from a host of schools that best fit their child's needs. And when parents exercise that choice, they should not be made to feel defensive about it. Instead, we should make sure that all parents are able to exercise the same privilege. To that point, here is an excerpt from one of my speeches on why school choice is so important:

> I have come to realize that each and every proposal for improving our schools is designed for the future, not now. Just pick one. Common core. Early childhood education.Local school district reform. All look to the future. What about the needs of children who we know are in bad schools today? This is why I have been such a strong advocate for educational choice. While we work to fix the system, what about that mom or dad who has to enroll their child in a school tomorrow and all they have are bad options? Folks seem to ignore that question. Interestingly, it is clear that the only people who are against educational choice are the ones who already have it. Be that as it may, because of educational choice options in the form of opportunity scholarships, tax credit scholarships, education savings accounts, charter schools, virtual schools, and home schooling, parents can get the immediate relief they want and need for their children. Those parents are saying to the leaders of the day the very same thing that Dr. King and those Birmingham children were saying to the leaders of the time: we can't wait; now is the time for you to recognize the

fierce urgency of now as it relates to our children's future. They need a high quality education today. The great tragedy is that while we wait, while we continue to move with "all deliberate speed" as states like Virginia did following the Brown v Board of Education ruling, we lose children—and their unknown potential. Who knows how many lawyers, doctors, artists, engineers, entrepreneurs and change agents were never produced because they never received the education that they deserved. Who knows how many cures of cancer are trapped inside the mind of a child we failed to educate?[6]

In DC, charter schools were working extremely well, far outpacing public schools in both popularity and results.[7] By 2003, there were thousands of DC children on waiting lists trying to enroll in a charter school.[8] By then, I was less vulnerable to the politics of education. Unfortunately, so much of lawmaking is done through the lens of party politics. But the party politics associated with education issues is particularly toxic. As one of the first Democrats in the nation embracing and driving the growth of charter schools, I had felt the ire of the teachers union and party colleagues urging me to back away from being strident in my support of charter schools. None of those urgings had an effect on me. I had seen the promise and hope restored in many families in my ward because one of their children got into a good charter school. For me, there was no turning back. I continued to support and fund the reforms at our public schools, but the immediate, short-term benefit of charter schools for low-income families inspired me. The problem was, however, that the waiting lists and lottery process was taking away the newfound hope from far too many families in need.

Notes

1. Ray Budde, *Education by Charter: Redistricting School Districts* (Andover: The Regional Laboratory for Educational Improvement of the Northeast & Islands, 1988), https://www.edreform.com/wp-content/uploads/2014/12/Education-by-Charter-Restructuring-School-Districts-Ray-Budde.pdf.
2. YilanShen and Alexander Berger, "Charter School Finance," National Conference of State Legislatures, February 2011, http://www.ncsl.org/documents/educ/charterschoolfinance.pdf.
3. "President Clinton and Charter Schools: A History Lesson," The Center for Education Reform, June 21, 2011, https://www.edreform.com/edspresso-shots/president-clinton-and-charter-schools-a-history-lesson/.
4. For enrollment numbers, please see: "Number and Enrollment of Public Elementary and Secondary Schools, by School Level, Type, and Charter and Magnet Status: Selected Years, 1990–91 through 2012–13," National

Center for Education Statistics, accessed December 30, 2015, https://nces.ed.gov/programs/digest/d14/tables/dt14_216.20.asp. For waitlist numbers, please see: Nora Kern and Wentana Gebru, "Waiting Lists to Attend Charter Schools Top 1 Million Names," National Alliance for Public Charter Schools, May 2014, http://www.publiccharters.org/wp-content/uploads/2014/05/NAPCS-2014-Wait-List-Report.pdf.

5. For articles that support this statement, please see the following articles: "How New York City's Charter Schools Affect Achievement," The New York City Charter Schools Evaluation Project, IV—1, September 2009. Joshua D. Angrist, Parag A. Pathak, and Christopher Walters, "Explaining Charter School Effectiveness," *American Economic Journal: Applied Economics* 5, no. 4 (2013): 1–27, http://economics.mit.edu/files/9102. Marianna Lombardo, "Charter Schools in Atlanta, Baltimore, Chicago and Miami: A NAEP Bright Spot for Low-Income Kids?," *Education Reform Now*, October 29, 2015, https://edreformnow.org/charter-schools-in-atlanta-baltimore-chicago-and-miami-a-naep-bright-spot-for-low-income-kids/. Joshua Angrist et al.,"Student Achievement in Massachusetts' Charter Schools," Center for Education Policy Research, Harvard University, January 2011, http://cepr.harvard.edu/files/cepr/files/cepr-ma-charter-schools.pdf?m=1429125531.

6. Kevin Chavous, Speech given at the School Choice Week Rally in Birmingham, Alabama, January 22, 2014.

7. "DC's Public Charter Schools: Reform That Works for DC's Most Underserved Children," FOCUS, accessed December 30, 2015 http://www.focusdc.org/charter-facts.

8. 149 Cong. Rec. 23,431 (2003).

8

School Vouchers in DC

I was fully immersed in my committee work in early 2003, when Howard Fuller called me and asked if I was open to having a conversation with Education Secretary Rod Paige about vouchers in DC. If there ever was a more toxic concept to Democratic party loyalists and folks associated with traditional public schools than school vouchers, I do not know what it is. No issue in education is as controversial or politically charged. The concept, standing alone, seems simple enough: School vouchers allow parents to receive scholarships to send their children to eligible private schools. These state scholarships are usually targeted to students who come from low-income families, have exceptional learning needs, or who currently attend failing public schools. Vouchers are funded through state tax dollars, allowing parents to "vote with their feet" and select the best schools for their children, public or private. Nationwide, there are twenty-one school voucher programs in existence, and research has demonstrated that vouchers increase student achievement, boost graduation rates, and can even help public schools improve. They have also led to high satisfaction rates in both students and parents.[1]

But none of that matters. For public school advocates, school vouchers—and the similar state tax credit scholarship concept—is all part of a grand design to destroy public schools and privatize education so that corporations can make money and profit in the kindergarten through high-school education arena.[2] In the mid-to-late 1990s, for those of us promoting reform and innovation in education, embracing charter schools was viewed as a huge political risk. Supporting school vouchers as a Democrat was considered political suicide.[3]

Having been through the school reform wars for several years—with the scars to prove it—I was probably more open to the idea than

I would have been when I first assumed control of the education committee in late 1996. But I was still wary of the politics, while not being held hostage by it. During that first call, as much as I respected, even revered Howard, I raised my concerns. "Howard," I said, "You know how much I have been killed in DC over charter schools. I have a hard enough time keeping my colleagues on the Council off of my back. I think vouchers are a non-starter, especially being pushed by President Bush. Plus, I don't think Mayor Williams will support vouchers." Howard, in his own patient, yet direct way, spoke eloquently about us having the opportunity to save more of our children by getting them in good schools and that fact alone made it worth having a conversation.

"Kevin, I do understand all of that," he said. "But we are all in this for the children, right? What is the harm of us sitting down to talk. I would like to facilitate a meeting between you, Mayor Anthony Williams and Secretary Paige—four African American men talking about ways we can educate more of our children. There is power in that and we should always be open to a conversation under those circumstances."

He then asked me to try to get Mayor Tony Williams to come to a meeting with him and Secretary Paige. Not only did I agree to the meeting, I also agreed to talk with Mayor Williams about attending it.

Here, I must say that there are very few people in my life who I respect and appreciate more than Dr. Howard Fuller. What a life! He was a basketball star growing up in Milwaukee and later became a black nationalist, where he spent time in Africa and then became an academic. He has a PhD in education and eventually became superintendent of schools in Milwaukee. While in that role, during the early 1990s, he led the fight to have the first voucher program enacted in the nation. An unprecedented move by a sitting public school superintendent. In 1999, he gathered together a group of African-American educators, activists, and concerned citizens to found the Black Alliance for Educational Options (BAEO). BAEO has been at the forefront of promoting educational choice options for low-income African Americans around the country ever since. If there were a Mount Rushmore dedicated to those key individuals who have advanced the cause of educational equality, Howard Fuller's face would be on it.

Dr. Fuller's stature notwithstanding, I had to give some serious thought to the purpose of the meeting. Over the previous several years, a group of Republican legislators had proposed a federal voucher bill for low-income DC residents. None of those representatives had reached out to city leaders to discuss the various proposals, and our DC delegate, Congresswoman Eleanor Holmes Norton, hated the Republicans and she hated vouchers. Each year, however, the proposal would surface and there was always a hearty band of DC parents, led by parent leader and BAEO cofounder Virginia Walden Ford, who would voice support.

Personally, I had always viewed vouchers as untenable because of the intense hostility they evoked among my fellow Democrats. As I told Howard, I was having a hard-enough time getting my folks on board with charters. Still, I called Mayor Anthony Williams to discuss Howard's request. And I was surprised at myself for feeling open to the idea. My relationship with Tony Williams had come a long way from our battle to become mayor. Our staffs had begun to work well together and we were in sync on education issues. Often, at the regular meetings with my colleagues on the council, Tony and I were on one side and everyone else was on the other. Eventually, we would usually win, and after a while folks understood that if he and I were together on an issue, we would generally get what we wanted. Our relationship had been further strengthened when I decided not to run for mayor again in 2002. Frankly, my heart wasn't in it, though my polling showed I could win. My chances had been elevated when I publicly fought the mayor over the closing of our public hospital, DC General. It was a clear hot button issue and I thought his policy was dead wrong. My supporters around the city were glad to see me take on that fight. But secretly, I realized that I had grown weary of the political back and forth. I wasn't even sure if I wanted to run for reelection in 2004. I knew that I would end up working in the education reform area post elective office. I just was not sure when that would be.

When I reached out to Tony about Howard's request, he hesitated, just as I had done. "I don't know about vouchers, Kevin," he said. "What do you think?"

"I told Howard the same thing, but I do agree with him that there is no harm in sitting down to talk."

Tony agreed to the meeting, but also wanted to make sure that it was not publicized. He said he would keep it off his official calendar. I shared Tony's perspective with Howard and the meeting was set up.

To say that the meeting was significant would be an understatement. Looking back on things now, I can say, without question, that our meeting and the resultant enactment of the DC Opportunity Scholarship Program (DCOSP) provided momentum for similar legislation in other states for the next several years. Our fight in DC also demystified the notion of vouchers; it took the horns off the issue. But it was not an easy undertaking.

When the four of us sat down, Tony and I immediately adopted a listening posture. Although we knew why we were there, we really wanted to hear Howard and the secretary make the case for something we expected we would not be able to support. In true Howard fashion, Howard began to talk about the plight of African-American children and the lack of urgency that most people attach to educating our children. He talked about our babies being faceless to far too many in power and that we all need to do more, irrespective of the personal cost. Then he launched into the obvious visual of the room. "Look at us," he said. "Here we are, four Black men trying to figure out the best way to educate our children. There ain't nobody else here but us. This is an in-the-family discussion and we should be able to find some common ground."

I could see the mayor squirming and I felt that I had to break Howard's stride, at least for Tony's sake. "Howard, we truly get all that you are saying, but there are so many dynamics at play. Republicans on the Hill have tried to ram this down our throat and that just won't work."

Of course, Howard wouldn't let me get away with my Republican reference. "Frankly, Kevin, this is not about the Republicans. You just heard the Secretary of Education say he would work with you to help your children. Who knows when we will have this opportunity in the future."

Mayor Williams, who had been mum for most of the meeting, said that he appreciated the offer to help us and that we should continue to talk. He emphasized that both he and I needed to be on the same page. I was surprised when he did not reject the idea, but, then again, neither did I.

We agreed to reconvene at some point soon and left. Little did I know that the mayor's press secretary, who did not support vouchers, was doing all he could to keep the mayor away from this issue. Somehow the press got wind of our meeting and I started to get calls from all the major news media. The mayor's press secretary issued a statement saying that the mayor does not support vouchers and made that fact clear to the secretary of education when the issue was broached. When I read that quote in the paper, I was stunned. I called Tony, who told me that his press folks jumped ahead of him on this. I then spoke with both Secretary Paige and Howard about the article. Despite the media reports, I realized that Tony was where I was: open to supporting vouchers. One factor that kept gnawing at me was making me more inclined to consider vouchers: the slow pace of reform within the public school system. With each passing year, we were continuing to lose children because of the bureaucracies' internal resistance to change. And while a good number of our charter schools were doing great, the waiting lists were now into the thousands.[4] Quite simply, our children needed more quality options and couldn't wait for public schools to provide them.

Soon after our meeting with Secretary Paige, Mayor Williams and I began to talk about what it would take to support vouchers. I zeroed in on the secretary's invitation to let him know what we needed to make this work. I told Tony that for the proposal to have traction, it made sense for there to be more to it than just vouchers. From there, we began noodling over the idea of having what we later called a "three-sector strategy." The original Bush administration proposal called for a federal voucher program designed so that up to two thousand children could attend select private schools on public dollars.[5] We suggested that in order to make this a true partnership that was intended to lift all boats, the Feds should give the same amount to DC public and charter schools. Secretary Paige and Howard both liked the "lift all boats" concept, and over the next couple of months I met with several Bush administration folks as well as local business leaders who supported the initiative. Still, the mayor and I played coy with the press and my colleagues about our discussions.

Finally, during charter school week in May 2003, the mayor and I announced that we were supporting vouchers in DC. Ironically, a big charter school event was scheduled at Kent Amos' Community Academy Charter School. The secretary and others had been waiting on us to make a decision. Right before the event was about to start, I pulled the mayor into Kent's private office and asked him what he was going to do. He said, "I don't know. What are you going to do?" We were like two little children trying to decide who would jump off the diving board first.

I then said, "Tony, let me ask you this. Do you believe that this is the right thing to do . . . that it would help some of our children?"

"Actually, Kevin, I do believe that."

"Then let's go out there and tell them we have worked it out with Secretary Paige and want it to happen."

As we both spoke in support of vouchers in DC, I could tell by the way the press was reacting that this was a big deal. Deep down, I don't believe that anyone thought we would actually do it. I immediately called DC Council chair, Linda Cropp, who was a dear friend. She always deferred to me in education matters and I needed to give her a heads up. She told me to buckle up and also to be careful: "Tony is the Mayor, so he has security. You don't!"

The firestorm was unleashed. Within days, the mayor and I were castigated by a wide range of people. DC Congresswoman Eleanor Holmes Norton and Senator Ted Kennedy held a press conference blasting me and the mayor by name for selling out to the Republicans. Congresswoman Norton then called me personally to give me a piece of her mind. I gave her a piece of mine in return. Then, several days later, she called me back. "Your Mayor is avoiding me," she blurted out when I picked up the phone.

"What are you talking about, Eleanor?" I asked.

"I said your Mayor is avoiding me. I have called his office several times to tell him what I think about this foolish deal you and he have made with the Republicans and he won't call me back. Now, he is sending his staff to public events where we both would normally attend. I know his a-- is avoiding me."

"Eleanor," I assured her, "I am confident that is not the case. Tell you what; I am going to go up to his office right now and have him call you."

I then hung up the phone and went directly to Mayor Tony Williams' office. When I was told by his staff that he was in a meeting, I told them that this was an emergency and that I needed to see him right away. After just a couple of minutes, Tony greeted me and took me to his private office, complete with the accountant's green lamp shade. (Unlike Marion Barry, Tony Williams was never comfortable with the ostentatious trappings of power. He eschewed the large, well-decorated ceremonial mayor's office for a small, windowless office that was sparsely decorated. It looked like, well, an accountant's office—and fit him to a T.)

We both sat down in chairs in which a credenza with a telephone was right between us. "Perfect set up," I thought.

"Tony," I began, "Our Congresswoman just called me. She says you are avoiding her because you know she is going to lay into you about us supporting vouchers. I told her that couldn't be the case and that I would have you call her."

Tony looked at me sheepishly.

"Well," he said. "I *am* avoiding her because I know she is going to yell at me. I don't want to get yelled at by her."

I was kind of floored. As good a mayor as Tony Williams ended up being, he still approached his job vastly different from most who run big cities. He never quite grasped that he was *the* man; that he had the power; and that every now and then, he had to use it. I decided to take that approach.

"Well, I understand that, Tony. She is going to yell at you, because that is how she is. She called me and yelled at me. I yelled back a little and now we are fine. But, Tony, you are the Mayor! You have the power! Eventually, she has to fall in line behind your leadership. You can easily back her up, Tony! You are the Mayor of the Nation's Capitol!"

Seeing that Tony wasn't buying it, I offered another approach.

"Let's do this, Tony," I said. "Let's call her right now and get this over with. I will be right here with you."

Hesitantly, he said ok.

I then dialed Eleanor's number with the phone between us on speaker. When the receptionist answered, Tony paused and looked at me. I looked back at him, pointing at the phone.

"Is Congresswoman Norton there? This is Mayor Tony Williams."

"Oh, well, yes," the young receptionist stammered. "Let me find her right away."

"At least the receptionist knows who has the power," I thought to myself.

After a few minutes of waiting, the receptionist finally came back to the phone. While waiting, Tony was looking nervous and anxious.

"Mr. Mayor," the receptionist said. "I am so sorry, but the Congresswoman went to a committee hearing. I tried to catch her, but I couldn't. Can I take a message? I will get it right to her."

Tony, looking relieved, said the following, "Yes, please. Tell her to call Councilman Chavous as soon as possible." He then abruptly hung up.

I just shook my head. We both were laughing as I left his office. Of course, eventually, he did talk with Eleanor. She did yell at him, and he did survive.

The negative opinions, however, did not end with Congress-woman Norton.

Late one night, my oldest son, Kevin, picked up the phone at my house, cupped the speaker, and told me that Senator Kennedy was on the phone. As soon as I said hello, the senator lit into me. "Kevin, what in the f--- do you think you are doing? How can you get in bed with those g--d--- Republicans? You and the Mayor must be out of your minds." He was yelling so loud that my son, who was still nearby, whispered, "Is that THE Senator Kennedy, the President's brother? Why is he cursing you out, dad?"

I took it for a while, but then I cut him off. "Senator, I have a lot of respect for you and your family and your contributions to our country. I also admire your steadfast commitment to DC statehood. But, with all due respect, Senator, you live in Boston. I would have no right calling your house late at night to tell you what you should do for your folks in Boston. And you certainly don't have any right calling my house late at night to tell me what to do for my folks here in southeast DC!"

I honestly do not think that Senator Ted Kennedy was used to anyone talking to him like that. After some silence, he finally said, "Well, Kevin, you are right about all of that." Pause. "But you are still wrong to be with those Republicans!"

Of course, it didn't end there. For the next several months, before the final vote, I was beat up on pretty badly by rank and file

Democrats. Interestingly, most of the heat came from national party types. Eleanor tried to rile up some of the folks in my ward, but most were ok with my actions. The mayor and I made it clear that we helped to create a unique one-of-a-kind partnership with the federal government that would end up contributing to all of our K-12 educational sectors. Charter schools would be able to use their money to leverage facility construction; public schools would have additional money for a use to be determined in the future (after over ten years, many still are not clear what they have done with the allotment); and up to one thousand seven hundred low-income children will be able to go to quality private schools—immediately.[6] Once my folks—especially parents—understood the proposal, they were fine with it.

Eventually, the school board president and a handful of other leaders stepped up in support of the three-sector strategy, but the ultimate vote on the Hill was still close.

The bill that encompassed our proposal passed the House of Representatives by one vote. Ironically, Representative Harold Ford from Tennessee was the only member of the Congressional Black Caucus to vote for our bill. Many others told me they would have voted for the bill had it not been for Congresswoman Norton's badgering. Harold's vote was truly a profile in courage. After the vote, I ran into his mother at a social event I attended. She had supported me in the past, but she must have been feeling the pressure as well. "What did you get my son into, Councilman? I am getting calls from everyone." She did mostly laugh it off. I got the sense that she was proud of his independence.

When the bill got to the Senate, Congresswoman Norton and Senator Kennedy were working hard to defeat it. We needed a few Democrats to vote for the bill, and Senator Mary Landrieu had intimated to me and the mayor that she would be supportive. Since she was a strong charter schools supporter, she especially liked the fact that charter schools were included in our bill. Then she went south on us. Senator Kennedy and her caucus got her to drop her expected support. Eventually, Joe Lieberman and Diane Feinstein became our champions and voted for the bill. Right before the vote, Eleanor verbally accosted Senator Feinstein, grabbed her arm, and told her that there was no way any true Democrat could support vouchers. Mayor Williams and I were watching the whole scene and were waiting to talk with the senator when Eleanor was finished. Then the mayor had to leave, and I went to talk with Senator Feinstein right after Eleanor finished her tirade. The senator immediately launched into me. "Your Congresswoman just left and is all over me about this bill. You and the Mayor need to tell me why I should support it." I started to talk about the three-sector approach; how it lifts all boats; and how, as a former mayor, she should understand why it is important to give deference to the local leaders dealing with these education issues on a daily basis. Then, I finally told her, "Senator, if there is one issue that this country should approach on a nonpartisan basis, it is education. This is an opportunity for you to cast a vote based on what you feel will ultimately serve the best interests of children in this city." Three days later, the senator wrote an editorial endorsing vouchers for the first time.

Notes

1. "Types of Educational Choice: School Vouchers," American Federation for Children, accessed December 30, 2015, http://www.federationforchildren. org/ed-choice-101/types-educational-choice/.

2. Examples of articles that support this point of view or highlight individuals who do include: David L. Kirp, "The Wrong Kind of Education Reform: Three New Books Decimate the Case for Charter Schools and Vouchers," Slate, September 4, 2013, http://www.slate.com/articles/news_and_politics/science/2013/09/charters_schools_and_vouchers_decimating_the_case_for_privatizing_public.html. And, "The Case against Vouchers," The National Education Association, accessed December 30, 2015, http://www.nea.org/home/19133.htm.

3. For examples that highlight the tense political climate around school vouchers at the time, please see: Charles Wheelan, "Democrats Stand in the Schoolhouse Door on Vouchers," The Philly, June 1, 1999, http://articles.philly.com/1999-06-01/news/25497629_1_school-choice-vouchers-public-schools. Or Michelle Rhee, My Break with the Democrats, excerpted from Michelle Rhee's book Radical: Fighting to Put Students First and republished by The Daily Beast, February 4, 2013, http://www.thedailybeast.com/articles/2013/02/04/michelle-rhee-my-break-with-the-democrats.html. Additionally, this recent press release from Congresswoman Eleanor Holmes Norton's website highlights that this is still a divisive topic today, https://norton.house.gov/media-center/press-releases/norton-to-testify-against-dc-voucher-bill-at-rules-committee-today-final.

4. 149 Cong. Rec. 23,431 (2003).

5. Jay Mathews, "Bush Pushes Vouchers, D.C. Charters,"*The Washington Post* Online, July 2, 2003, https://www.washingtonpost.com/archive/politics/2003/07/02/bush-pushes-vouchers-dc-charters/3100af21-42f8-40d8-8641-1be2cd432a56/.

6. Spenser S. Hsu, "How Vouchers Came to D.C.,"*EducationNext* 4, no. 4 (Fall, 2004), http://educationnext.org/howvoucherscametodc/.

9

Losing My Council Seat and Joining the Education Reform Movement

Once the DC Opportunity Scholarship Program (DCOSP) bill ultimately passed, many Democrats and education establishment types were stunned. They continued to berate me.

It was clear that my support of the DCOSP voucher program unearthed an unheard of hostility and vitriol. And as council chair Linda Cropp reminded me, unlike the mayor, I had no security. Union reps began to follow me around at my various public events to heckle me; they obtained permits to picket in front of my house; garbage was thrown on my front porch and thousands of negative flyers were placed in the tree branches in my yard and the yards of nearby neighbors on my block. In the spring of 2004, I released my first book, *Serving Our Children: Charter Schools and the Reform of American Public Education*. The hecklers were out in force at my book launch party held at the City Museum across from the DC Convention Center. They harassed each of the attendees as they walked in and out of the event. According to some in the DC education establishment, I was public enemy number one and I was running for reelection that year which made me a clear target. The passage of the DCOSP sealed my decision to run for another term. I already had had some concerns about charters getting attacked. I felt I needed to be there to help protect our educational choice options in the District. But my time in office had run its course.

I recall one eerie and disturbing encounter with a longtime supporter and well-known city activist. We were at a reception in Georgetown that contained a rather upscale crowd. I noticed that the woman was staring at me from across the room. She was holding a glass of wine and while she was looking at me with a half smile, her hand began to shake, so much so that she started to spill her wine. I was talking with a group of people, so I just looked away. Some time later, when I was finally alone, I turned around and she was right in my face, still holding her wine, with evidence of the spill on the sleeve of her blouse. I called her name, said hello, and asked if she was alright. She then put down her wine glass, grabbed my hand with both of her hands, and slowly began to squeeze my hand as she spoke.

"Councilman, I have always supported you; always believed that you were part of the future of the city," she said in a very soft, but strong voice. "But I now detest you for supporting vouchers. I absolutely detest you." By now, she was squeezing my hand harder and her lips were quivering, almost as if she were having a seizure.

"And know this," she continued. "I will do everything in my power to destroy you. Do you understand? I will do everything in my power to bring you down."

For some reason, I was totally nonplussed and unflappable in spite of her behavior. "Ma'am," I said, "I appreciate your support over the years and understand that you have to do what you have to do. But, I would have had more respect for you if you had at least once mentioned the children I am trying to help. The mere fact that you can come at me the way you have and get worked up over the politics, with no mention of the children, tells me that I more than did the right thing, because all I care about are our children, not the politics. So please, do what you have to do."

While I did lose my bid for a fourth term on the DC Council, my stand on education reform and educational choice was not the main reason why I lost. While the issue did fortify my political opponents, I was not reelected because I had lost touch with the immediate day-to-day needs of my constituents. I had become a one-note Johnny: all I talked about and most of what I gave my attention to related to education issues. As is the case in many working-class communities, the folks in my ward wanted me to pay attention to their immediate needs: crime, housing, city services, development. They grew tired of me waxing on and on about the education of our children. That reality hit me squarely as I was campaigning door to door in a high voter precinct where I historically had support.

I noticed that my opponent's yard sign was on the front lawn of one of my longtime supporters. This supporter was highly influential in my ward and he owned a huge corner lot. I knew that not having his support meant that I was in trouble, so I walked up his driveway and knocked on his door. He opened the door with a frown on his face (not good) and proceeded to lay into me.

"Chavous, I know why you are here and I still think you are a good guy," he said. "But you spend too much time talking about education and those damn children! Most of us are retired and yeah, we care about the schools, but we care more about getting our alleys cleaned and the city picking up the trash on time. We feel like you aren't focused on our needs."

I thought about what he said for a moment and then I grabbed his hand. "You know," I said. "You are so right. I have been totally focused on education issues, because I do believe that fixing our schools will ultimately fix most of our neighborhood problems. And honestly, that is where my interests are and what I feel my calling is. I can also tell you that my focus probably won't change, but I thank you so much for believing in me over the years."

He did smile and give me a hug before I left his doorstep, but I knew I had lost his vote and the election, the third best thing to happen to me during my political career in DC. The best thing that ever happened to me was my first win. It allowed me to serve the city that I loved and to impact on public policy in a way longed for by many. I will always be eternally grateful to my neighbors in southeast and northeast DC to have the honor of representing them.

The second best thing to happen to me during my political career was running for mayor and then losing that race. Yes, I believe I would have been a good mayor, but, looking back, the city needed the fresh start that it got from Tony Williams. More than that, however, it allowed me to give all of my focus to the education issues facing the city. Following the mayor's race, I aggressively worked to recruit high-quality charter schools to the city and continued to populate their boards with key city influencers, partnered with American University to develop a landmark early childhood education report, which has been followed by many jurisdictions around the country; helped to stabilize the University of the District of Columbia and its law school when there was an aggressive attempt to close it; and helped to spearhead the development of the DCOSP. I also helped to keep reform moving within DC public schools. As long as I was the education committee chair, public school officials knew they could not be complacent; they knew I would push them. Finally, I drove new school construction in a town that hadn't built a new school in nearly twenty years. Using the city's capital budget, I was able to fund a host of brand new schools (both public and charter schools), libraries, and recreation centers.

But all of those initiatives did come with some political cost. It became evident to the education establishment that I was not going to go along to get along. As a result, I often ran counter to the political stereotypes. Interestingly, as I pushed more aggressively for change and seemed to get more demonstrative opposition (hecklers, vicious mail, etc.), I also received more heartfelt thank-yous from parents along with increasing private support from folks within the status quo. As I was to later discover during visits around the country, so many people in education want change but are afraid to step out in front. The same holds true for many politicians. Charter schools, education reform, and educational choice have mistakenly been viewed as Republican Party issues. Yet, those issues acutely impact vastly more Democratic constituents. When I lost my last election in 2004, it became clear to me that the party label was a barrier to clear-thinking, commonsense education policy proposals. I ruminated over ways that we could engage members of the Democratic Party to look at education through the lens of parents and children and not through the lens of party politics. That internal thinking is what led to Democrats for Education Reform (DFER).

Much has been written and said about the origins of DFER, a DC-based policy organization that has pushed the Democratic Party more to the center on education issues. Folks like Diane Ravitch and Randi Weingarten have used DFER to help with their billionaire bullies narrative, saying that NY hedge fund billionaires support DFER as part of their new "favorite fad."[1] Yet all of this information is misleading and dead wrong. I should know, because DFER was my brainchild. My vision was to have an organization founded and funded by Democrats that could weigh in on education issues and support candidates for office who have the courage to step away from the union-driven establishment party line to do what's best for children. Check out this excerpt from DFER's Statement of Principles:

> Both political parties have failed to address the tragic decline of our system of public education, but it is the Democratic Party—our party—which must question how we allowed ourselves to drift so far from our mission. Fighting on behalf of our nation's most vulnerable individuals is what our party is supposed to stand for. DFER aims to return the Democratic Party to its rightful place as a champion of children, first and foremost, in America's public education systems.[2]

In order to make this idea work, I needed resources. Through my good friend and hero, Howard Fuller, I eventually met New Yorkers Boykin Curry, Whitney Tilson, and John Petry, who helped me start DFER. We had our coming-out party at the 2008 National Democratic Convention in Denver. At our event, several big city mayors attended along with elected officials from all over the country. Folks like Denver Public Schools Superintendent (now US Senator) Michael Bennet, New York City Chancellor of Education Joel Klein, Cory Booker, and Al Sharpton all attended and spoke. After Senator Barack Obama was elected president, DFER's tentacles were evident during the transition. Our folks helped to influence the selection of Arne Duncan as secretary of education. Today, DFER is more than living up to its mission and I am very proud of DFER's leader, Executive Director Shavar Jeffries. We clearly need to take the politics out of education, and one of the most effective tools in doing that is to have political organizations like DFER continue to drive the message that our priorities have to be with parents and children.

The morning after my primary defeat in 2004, I got a call from Jeanne Allen, founder of the Center for Education Reform. "Kevin," she said, "I feel awful about your defeat. But DC's loss is the nation's gain. I want you to be a Distinguished Fellow with us and help us push reform around the country."

Howard Fuller then called and said he wanted me to get more involved with BAEO and its board.

Then the Alliance for School Choice called, as did several others with speaking engagements. That marked the beginning of the rest of my life doing the work I was called to do. Since that primary election loss, I have been completely immersed in the education reform and educational choice movement in America. Initially,

I did much of my work through my law firm SNR Denton. Then I worked with several Alliance for School Choice supporters to help found the American Federation for Children (AFC), now the nation's leading voice for school choice. AFC has been a perfect fit for me. The AFC board members have all been tireless advocates for children, and many have been dear friends. Everyone associated with the organization cares deeply about our children. I love working with the entire team there and I couldn't be happier. But my impatience, sense of urgency, and frustration persist. I cannot accept the fact that in the greatest nation on earth, nearly half of its children will wake up tomorrow and walk into the doors of a school that does not serve their needs. That fact alone keeps a fire burning in me. That fire fuels my work.

Since 2005, I have been to almost every state, given keynote speeches at nearly every state charter school conference, and written scores of articles and op-eds published by most major newspapers in the country. I have also appeared on countless local and national television programs, and I am now considered a leading national advocate of educational or school choice.

Often, I am asked why I am so passionate about school choice. The answer to that question lies within the school choice definition:

> School choice can be best defined as empowering parents to select the educational environment they feel is best for their child. In other words, school choice is parental choice. Some families are already able to exercise school choice simply because they have the resources to move to the neighborhood of their choice or to pay private school tuition. Families that do not have these same resources can only exercise choice through the use of different school choice tools, such as vouchers and tuition tax-credits.
>
> The best school choice tools are programs (like vouchers or tuition tax credits) in which education funds follow the child to the school of their parents' choice, whether public or private. Other school choice options include charter schools, private schools, open enrollment, magnet schools, virtual schools (including both public and private), privately-funded scholarships, and home schooling.[3]

To me, it is only through school choice that we can help families of need get their children in good schools immediately, without having to wait for the system to change. It is only through school choice that we can address the sense of urgency for those children and their families. Unfortunately, most education policymakers do not have the same sense of urgency to help these families that I do. They are totally comfortable with studying the study, planning the plan, and debating the debate approach to education reform while far too many of our children languish in underperforming schools. And while I remain mystified why the sense of urgency that I have about our children education is not more common, it is infinitely clear to me that the only people who are against school choice are the ones who already have it. And many of those folks are not as concerned about the empowerment of those parents who are less fortunate.

Someone who has shared my sense of urgency about making education work for all children is former New York City Schools Chancellor Joel Klein. Joel and I bonded nearly as soon as we met—both of us commiserating over the slow pace of reform. Joel instituted many needed reforms in New York, but, like me, he was always seeking to find a way to gain broader mainstream appeal for education reform. Joel also understood that our movement needed more high-profile faces of color in it. In 2008, Joel called me to ask if I would consider being part of a new entity he was putting together that would highlight and promote education reform. The group would be bipartisan and the cochairs would be Joel and Reverend Al Sharpton. Joel had been courting Rev. Sharpton about becoming a more vocal advocate for education reform. The new entity was titled the Education Equality Project (EEP). Joel asked me to be the president of the EEP Action Fund. Along with Joel and Rev. Sharpton, the EEP board included folks like Howard Fuller and Joe Williams, the former head of DFER. Singer John Legend also later joined the board. Soon EEP's list of supporters was a who's who of major political and education reform leaders. Folks like Jeb Bush, Michelle Rhee, Cory Booker, Los Angeles Mayor Antonio Villaraigosa, Newt Gingrich, Adrian Fenty, and United Negro College Fund's CEO Michael Lomax were all EEP signatories. From 2008 to 2011, EEP began convening diverse groups of influential leaders from around the United States to improve the American public education system. They organized numerous events focused on finding a solution to close the achievement gap, attracting leaders from communities of color, education experts, elected leaders, policy experts, and a support community of over seventy thousand individuals. EEP used strategic media, research, advocacy, and social media to shine a continual bright light on the achievement gap.

At the 2009 Obama inauguration, many of us gathered at DC's Cardozo High School for a rally calling for the new president to give education reform the attention it deserves. The event was emceed by both Joel and Rev. Sharpton. I spoke at the event, as did many others, including John McCain, despite being fresh off his presidential loss to Barack Obama.

A couple of months later, Joel got many of us together to speak at Rev. Sharpton's National Action Network Conference in Memphis. I was on a panel with Howard Fuller, Michelle Rhee, Adrian Fenty, and Urban League President Marc Morial. Later, we decided that we would have a huge rally in DC in May to commemorate the fifty-fifth anniversary of *Brown v. Board of Education*.

Leading up to the rally, I was in full throttle trying to get President Obama and Education Secretary Arne Duncan to reinstate the DCOSP scholarships for the 216 children they took them from. I had been leading protests and rallies against the president on this issue. The day before the rally, Al Sharpton, Newt Gingrich, and Joel Klein all met with the president and Secretary Duncan at the White House to discuss education reform in general. Gingrich and Sharpton were beginning to get a lot of "odd couple" press coverage around their joining forces to promote education reform.

When I arrived on the mall near the Washington Monument for the rally, I was disappointed to see the sparse crowd. We knew that C-Span would cover the rally live, but Rev. Sharpton was supposed to get folks there from all over the country. Frankly, most of the couple of thousand folks in attendance were the people I and Virginia Walden Ford had organized for our DCOSP rallies. In the VIP tent for speakers, I asked Joel about the crowd. He just said that it was Rev. Sharpton's responsibility and that he had been promised that more buses were coming. Needless to say, the buses never arrived.

Rev. Sharpton was the emcee and, one by one, he began to introduce speakers to the stage. As Rev. Sharpton was shuttling back and forth between the stage and the VIP tent, I noticed some agitation between him and Joel. Then folks started to look at me. Finally, Joel pulled me aside.

"Kevin," he said, almost embarrassedly, "Al doesn't want you to speak. He says you will be talking about vouchers and he won't allow that at this rally."

I was shocked. I knew that Rev. Sharpton had not embraced vouchers, but he also continued to talk about being more open to new ideas designed to help address our children's needs. In fact, he had noticeably backed away from his antichoice rhetoric since he had been working with Joel.

"What did you say to him, Joel?" I asked firmly.

Without missing a beat, Joel said, "I told Al that if you don't speak, I won't speak. This is your city, your people are out there and you have been a leader in fighting for children."

I was numb. Joel was, indeed, a true mensch.

"What did he say to that, Joel?"

"He tried to push back, but I think he was surprised. I think he is going to try to rally other speakers against you," Joel said.

Sure enough, several other speakers started to come to me about Rev. Sharpton. Even Newt Gingrich, who I got to know pretty well when he was Speaker of the House. Gingrich approached me and was very clear. "Kevin, Rev. Al doesn't want you to speak, because of vouchers. You know I support vouchers and I support your work. I told him if you don't speak, I won't speak."

And so it went. Speaker after speaker told Rev. Sharpton the same thing. Rev. Sharpton was thrown off stride. He was not expecting the speakers to support me in the way that they did. Since I am more of a direct approach guy, I decided to speak directly with Rev. Sharpton. That too surprised him.

"Rev. Sharpton," I said, "Why are you trying to stop me from speaking?"

He never looked at me in the eyes, only looking away while answering. "It's not me, Kevin," he said. "We were at the White House yesterday, and you know the president doesn't support vouchers. Arne Duncan said they didn't want you to speak. I have to support the president."

I then went straight to Arne Duncan.

"Arne, Rev. Sharpton says you and the president don't want me to speak today. Why not?"

Arne Duncan looked stunned. "We never said that, Kevin," he said. "We never said that at all."

In the end, I did speak. Rev. Sharpton had no choice. As a result of all the drama, I did adjust my speech accordingly. I added *more* emphasis on the need for vouchers and private school choice than I had originally planned—just for the benefit of any and all who may be watching on C-Span.

Notes

1. Steven Brill, *Class Warfare: Inside the Fight to Fix America's Schools* (New York: Simon & Schuster, 2011), 302, 322.
2. "Statement of Principles," Democrats for Education Reform, accessed December 30, 2015, http://dfer.org/about-us/statement-of-principles/.
3. "School Choice Info: What Is School Choice?," Parents for Choice in Education, accessed December 30, 2015, http://www.choiceineducation. org/schoolchoice_faq.php.

10

Glimmers of Hope

Fortunately, in spite of the politics there are glimmers of hope found in schools and approaches that do work for all children. Some of those examples are found in traditional schools, some in alternative schools. Still, from my vantage point, the biggest driver for change has been the growing popularity of educational choice programs, of every form. Quite simply, in its purest form, educational choice means allow for the transference of power from school district to parent. Through a robust array of educational service options from which to choose, parents, particularly low-income parents, no longer are limited to the school "assigned" to them for their child. Through choice, parents have the power to pick the best educational setting for their children that works for them.

Over the past two decades, charter schools have grown in number and attendance. In 2008, only 3 percent of all public school students attended charter schools, yet that number increased greatly over the previous decade. In 1999, there were 1,542 charter schools with 349,642 students, but by 2008, the numbers had grown to 4,618 charter schools with 1,407,817 students.[1] Looking at DC in particular, the numbers of students attending charter schools have risen to nearly comparable numbers in public schools, with 37,684 students attending public charter schools and 47,548 attending DC public schools.[2] Further, nationwide there are also now over 351,000 children who benefit from tax credit scholarships or vouchers that allow them to attend a private school. But it has been a fight every step of the way to achieve those numbers.

Of course, there have been examples of hope found in the reform efforts in certain states, particularly in states that have advanced more quality educational choice options for their children. The *Wall Street Journal* called 2011 the year of school choice because of all of the various educational choice measures popping up in various states.[3] It is noteworthy that even more such proposals emerged in 2012, 2013, and 2014.[4] In spite of all of the partisanship and rancor, many state legislators keep pushing to expand these options for children. Why? Because we still have too many schools that do not serve our children's needs and because parents are ready for a change, even if the leaders are not. Because of the laws forcing parents to send their children to their neighborhood school—even if that school is failing—many parents have no idea what innovation and creativity in schools look like. But they are ready to find out. As the quality of options grows from state to state, parents and students are gaining exposure to a new vision of what education can offer. This foundational knowledge builds the perfect platform for our new culture of learning.[5]

As we look around the country, there are jurisdictions using educational choice programs as a way to educate children that otherwise would not be educated. The results in these states demonstrate that not only does educational choice give parents immediate relief, but it also helps to drive change within the local traditional school system.

Florida has done a great job of offering a host of options to its residents by way of its corporate tax credit scholarship program—in which nearly eighty thousand low-income children received scholarships to private schools this year, a robust offering of charter schools along with easy access to virtual and blended learning, and nearly an increase of ten thousand students over last school year.[6]

In our nation's Capitol, public schools had finally begun to show improvement under the leadership of Chancellor Kaya Henderson, who has been able to navigate the politics of the city better than her well-intentioned predecessor, Michelle Rhee. Both extol the virtues of providing parents with quality options before waiting for the system to fix itself. Because DC charter schools and the DCOSP schools are popular and doing a great job of educating thousands of DC children, the public school system continues to have to up its game. In July 2014, the *Washington Post* reported on DC public school principals going door to door in an effort to lure families with children in charter schools to come back and enroll in public schools and to give them another chance. These principals had been trained by former Obama campaign field workers.[7] Now, of course, those campaign workers could not attest one way or another to whether the public schools were better. In fact, positive strides have been made by Chancellor Henderson. But it is refreshing to see that a local school district feels *compelled* to have to compete for students. Good stuff!

I am also proud of the progress that has been made in my home state of Indiana. The state has one of the best charter school laws in the country, which includes the unique aspect of allowing the mayor of Indianapolis to authorize new charter schools. Indiana also has legislatively broken down some of the barriers to virtual learning, making it easier for students to gain access to online course providers. Finally, Indiana has the most robust statewide scholarship program in the country. Over thirty thousand children are now enrolled in private schools with public dollars. The popular program has also led to more competition between the various educational service delivery providers. Recognizing the threat coming from these providers, Indianapolis public schools (IPS) took an approach similar to the DC public school system's approach and began to run billboard advertisements boasting to parents that the public schools too could give children a great education.[8]

Great strides toward reform have taken place in other states such as Arizona, which introduced the unique Education Savings Accounts (ESAs) to go along with its charter school offerings and its state tax credit scholarship program.[9] ESAs are private accounts managed by parents for use on educational expenses for their child. The state department of education calculates a per-pupil amount through the state's finance formula and makes quarterly deposits into the accounts. Parents can use account funds to purchase private school tuition, tutoring services, books and other materials, or even save for college. In 2015, Nevada passed the most sweeping ESA legislation in the country. Of Nevada's school-age children, 93 percent are eligible to receive an ESA.[10] Legislation offering this new form of educational choice is being offered in states all over the country.[11]

Many states have shown signs of embracing reform. However, as is the case everywhere, the legislative battles for change can be arduous and lengthy. One thing, however, is certain: where there is greater transparency for parents, there is a greater likelihood that the local school district will become more responsive to student needs.[12]

With each of these successes, however, efforts to roll them back continue to take place. Countless lawsuits and regressive counter legislation has served to limit the effectiveness of educational choice programs around the country.[13]

A little bit here, a little bit there. Two steps forward, one step back. That seems to be the reality for the education reform movement. Could it be that we have put too much focus on the systems we want to change as opposed to the people we want to learn?

*   *   *

Without question, the poster child for education reform—with a strong focus on changing the system—is the state of Louisiana, most notably New Orleans. Education Secretary Arne Duncan called Hurricane Katrina "the best thing that happened to the education system in New Orleans."[14] Before the hurricane, New Orleans was one of the worst performing school districts in America.[15] The greed I referred to that existed on the DC school board paled in comparison to the corruption which existed on the New Orleans school board prior to Katrina. Several board members went to jail and most would agree that the children were better off as a result. Today, without question, the children are doing better and are learning far more than they were under the old system.[16] In 2008, the Louisiana legislature passed a scholarship bill to allow low-income children to attend private school on public funds. I led a team that worked with Governor Bobby Jindal, State Senator Ann Duplessis, and Representative Austin Badon to get that bill passed. One of the challenges was bringing together people who normally don't work with each other on many issues. At first, it seemed as though Governor Jindal was especially uncomfortable working on both sides of the aisle. Soon, however, the governor was meeting with New Orleans parents and had forged a strong working relationship with Senator Duplessis. Without that level of collaboration, the bill would have never passed. That program worked so well that in 2012, the legislature expanded it statewide. And as of 2011, Louisiana's low-income residents had more educational choices for their children than most other places in the country.[17] The challenge is to make sure that these programs continue to grow and thrive.

In spite of all of the obvious academic success we see in New Orleans, far too many residents don't feel as though they are a part of it. In 2014, Howard Fuller took it upon himself to interview an assorted number of African-American New Orleans residents to get their views about the school reforms in their city. As reported to Howard, some locals he interviewed grudgingly acknowledged the improvements, but all complained about feeling put upon, invaded, and disrespected. In the one American city where reform seemingly flourishes, too many people do not feel as though they are a part of the change. Similar feelings exist in nearly every city where aggressive education reform has been initiated. Almost like the bureaucratic system it is trying to change, the education reform movement has fallen prey to the same top-down approaches that, frankly, more often than not rub people the wrong way. Far too frequently we are winning legislative battles for change, but losing the war to win over hearts and minds. All of this begs the question: How do we make changes to education work for children in a way that people can accept? How do we win the hearts and minds of the people we seek to serve?

Well, maybe the answer lies in our ultimate goal and in our approach. For the last twenty years we have had legislative battles over charter school legislation, tax credit scholarship bills, vouchers, teacher evaluations, performance pay proposals, tenure reform, accountability for principals, smaller class sizes, national standards, and so on. And while charter schools get a lot of attention and press, again, as of 2013 they still made up only 4.6 percent of the nation's 49 million public school children, a million of which are on charter school wait lists.[18] In addition, there are just over three hundred and eight thousand children who have publicly funded scholarships to attend private schools. And these paltry numbers exist despite the fact that there is overwhelming demand for more of these quality options, with over a million children on charter school waiting lists who could greatly benefit from more options.[19] For the parents who have been fortunate enough to have availed themselves of these options, getting their children a good educations has been life-changing. But we need more options for other parents in similar situations. Beyond the legislative battles, we need a spark, a catalyst to jumpstart broader change.

Notes

1. "Charter Schools: Finding Out the Facts: At a Glance, Charter Schools across the Nation," Center for Public Education, accessed January 2, 2016, http://www.centerforpubliceducation.org/Main-Menu/Organizing-a-school/Charter-schools-Finding-out-the-facts-At-a-glance#sthash.PbH43442.dpuf.

2. Historical Enrollment—Public Schools: 1967–2015 Public School Enrollment in the District," DC Public Charter School Board, accessed January 2, 2016, https://data.dcpcsb.org/Enrollment-/Historial-Enrollment-Public-Schools/3db5-ujzr.

3. "The Year of School Choice: No Fewer Than 13 States Have Passed Major Education Reforms," *The Wall Street Journal* Online, July 5, 2011, http://www.wsj.com/articles/SB10001424052702304450604576420330972531442.

4. *School Choice Yearbook 2011–2012*, Alliance for School Choice, accessed January 2, 2016, 11, http://issuu.com/afc.yearbooks/docs/school_choice_yearbook_2011-12; *School Choice Yearbook 2012–2013*, Alliance for School Choice, accessed January 2, 2016, 13, http://issuu.com/afc.yearbooks/docs/school_choice_yearbook_2012-13; *School Choice Yearbook 2013–2014*, Alliance for School Choice, accessed January 2, 2016, 15, http://issuu.com/afc.yearbooks/docs/afc_2013-14_yearbook.

5. *The Elements of Change: The Education Trust 2013 Annual Report*, accessed January 2, 2016, http://2013annualreport.edtrust.org.

6. "Florida's Tax Credit Scholarship Program Participation," Friedman Foundation for Education Choice, accessed January 2, 2016, http://www.edchoice.org/school-choice/programs/Florida-Tax-Credit-Scholarship-Program/.

7. Mike DeBonis, "Fishing for DCPS Students," *The Washington Post* Online, July 2, 2014, https://www.washingtonpost.com/blogs/mike-debonis/wp/2014/07/02/fishing-for-dcps-students/.

8. Tom Coyne, "Indiana Public Schools Wage Unusual Ad Campaign to Keep Students from Leaving for Private Schools in Voucher Program," *The Huffington Post*, August 20, 2012, http://www.huffingtonpost.com/2012/08/20/indiana-public-schools-wa_0_n_1813143.html.

9. "Welcome to ESA," Arizona Department of Education, accessed January 2, 2016, http://www.azed.gov/esa/.

10. Michael Chartier, "Everything You Need to Know about Nevada's Universal ESA Bill," Friedman Foundation for Educational Choice, accessed January 2, 2016, http://www.edchoice.org/everything-you-need-to-know-about-nevadas-universal-esa-bill/.

11. Jonathan Butcher, "Nevada's Education Gambit," *US News*, June 17, 2015, http://www.usnews.com/opinion/knowledge-bank/2015/06/17/nevadas-new-education-savings-accounts-will-give-parents-lots-of-options.

12. *The Elements of Change: The Education Trust 2013 Annual Report*, accessed January 2, 2016, http://2013annualreport.edtrust.org.

13. For examples of such counter-legislation and lawsuits, please see Neal Morton, "Judge May Rule Soon on Lawsuit Challenging Nevada Education Savings Accounts," *Las Vegas Review-Journal*, December 10, 2015, http://www.reviewjournal.com/news/education/judge-may-rule-soon-lawsuit

-challenging-nevada-education-savings-accounts and Stephanie Simon, "States Weigh Turning Education Funds Over to Parents,"*Politico* Online, February 6, 2015, http://www.politico.com/story/2015/02/state-education-savings-accounts-taxpayers-114966.

14.   Nick Anderson, "Education Secretary Duncan Calls Hurricane Katrina Good for New Orleans Schools,"*The Washington Post* Online, January 30, 2010, http://www.washingtonpost.com/wp-dyn/content/article/2010/01/29/AR2010012903259.html.

15.   "New Orleans Public Schools Pre-Katrina and Now, by the Numbers," nola.com, August 29, 2014, http://www.nola.com/education/index.ssf/2014/08/new_orleans_public_schools_pre.html.

16.   For articles that support this statement, please see: Douglas Harris, "Good News for New Orleans,"*EducationNext* 15, no. 4 (Fall 2015), http://educationnext.org/good-news-new-orleans-evidence-reform-student-achievement/. "The State of Public Education in New Orleans: Five Years after Hurricane Katrina," Cowen Institute for Public Education Initiatives, Tulane University, July 2010, 18–20, http://www.coweninstitute.com/wp-content/uploads/2010/07/katrina-book.final_.CIpageSmaller.pdf."The State of Public Education in New Orleans: 10 Years after Hurricane Katrina," Cowen Institute for Public Education Initiatives, Tulane University, June 2015, 18–22, http://www.speno2015.com/images/SPENO.2015.small.single.pdf."Recovery School District Fact Sheet," Louisiana Department of Education, accessed March 11, 2016, https://www.louisianabelieves.com/docs/default-source/katrina/final-louisana-believes-v8-recovery-school-district.pdf?sfvrsn=2. Christen Holly, et al.," Ten Years in New Orleans: Public School Resurgence and the Path Ahead," New Schools for New Orleans and Public Impact, 2015, 3, http://www.newschoolsforneworleans.org/wp-content/uploads/2015/06/Public-School-Resurgence-Executive-Summary-FINAL.pdf.

17.   Lindsey Burke and Rachel Sheffield, "School Choice in America 2011: Educational Opportunity Reaches New Heights," The Heritage Foundation, http://www.heritage.org/research/reports/2011/08/school-choice-in-america-2011-educational-opportunity-reaches-new-heights.

18.   "Number and Enrollment of Public Elementary and Secondary Schools, by School Level, Type, and Charter and Magnet Status: Selected Years, 1990–91 through 2012–13, https://nces.ed.gov/programs/digest/d14/tables/dt14_216.20.asp, and Nora Kern and Wentana Gebru, "Waiting Lists to Attend Charter Schools Top 1 Million Names," National Alliance for Public Charter Schools, May 2014, http://www.publiccharters.org/wp-content/uploads/2014/05/NAPCS-2014-Wait-List-Report.pdf.

19.   Nora Kern and Wentana Gebru, "Waiting Lists to Attend Charter Schools Top 1 Million Names," National Alliance for Public Charter Schools, May 2014, http://www.publiccharters.org/wp-content/uploads/2014/05/NAPCS-2014-Wait-List-Report.pdf.

Part 2

Achieving Reform: Building a Learning Culture in America

Introduction

The previous several chapters were purposely written from the perspective of someone deeply embroiled in the fight for change in our schools. As a result, I shared much of the political wrangling back and forth and some of the inside political maneuvering that I was involved in while in public office trying to promote an education reform agenda. In reflecting back on that time, as well as considering my current work in various states trying to get educational choice legislation passed, having to deal with the politics can be all encompassing. In that world, it is so easy to adopt the us versus them mindset. It is natural to be poised for the fight. Since taking over the chairmanship of the DC Council education committee in the late 1990s, it is the only perspective that made sense to me: that changes in education will never take place unless we are willing to fight for them—for our children. I still believe in education reform and I still believe in the transformative power of school choice, but what if we don't have to fight? What if our tedious and laborious focus on systemic change has led to our missing the forest for the trees? What if we could inspire all Americans to want to learn in a way that they won't feel as though they must pick sides in a fight?

Like the well-intentioned politician (myself included) who has lost touch with the people he or she serves, those of us who have been involved in setting education policy or running school districts are, for the most part, out of touch with the practical needs of the parents and their kids. Of course, there are exceptions, but by and large, we have unwittingly created a certain toxicity around education and learning. Often, as I give speeches throughout America, I am approached by parents with specific questions about their child's circumstances. Sadly, many of these parents feel overwhelmed by the school district bureaucracy and they often have no idea how to break through it. If one doesn't understand or speak government-speak, you are lost, and so may be your child. Frustration leads to hopelessness, which then leads to despair. It is almost as if we have depersonalized the most personal of government functions—educating our nation's children. To make matters worse, the schools in the communities with the most needs seem to fall prey to this phenomenon more than others. In far too many cases, the individual needs of children are practically subservient to the interests of the system.

But that's not all. As much as I enjoyed being a local legislator, I did not enjoy the hours and hours of political debate and maneuvering driven by politics. In the midst of some of these marathon discussions, often fueled by the politics of the day, I was frequently angered when internal political positioning and personal conflicts steered me and my colleagues away from meaningful topics that made a real difference in the lives of everyday people. Having seen legislative debates in assorted statehouses across the nation, I have come to believe that the politics surrounding education is as intense as it gets. In the political world, positioning and "who gets credit" mean nearly everything. So does political party leadership. Over the past several years, I have grown more and more weary watching state leaders vacillate, change their votes, and cut political deals that went against the interests of children. Unfortunately, when the political lens is attached to an issue, that lens can eventually become more important than the issue itself. Increasingly, I have come to believe that ultimately education laws birthed in a political environment cannot be longstanding. At some point, someone will try to change the law, repeal it, or replace it. That is what happens in politics and we have allowed politics to dominate our decision-making process on how we shape education policy. But what if we changed our focus? What if we made the politics of the day less of a priority on education-related matters? What if we shifted so much of our focus away from school systems? Or even schools?

Throughout my journey working to improve education in our nation's capital and beyond, my focus has been the same as everyone else who is associated with K-12 education in America—schools. Everything we do in education has to do with schools. How do we fix them? How do we change them? How do we close the bad ones? How do we get more children into the good ones? How do we replicate the good ones? And also, school systems. How do we save the school system? How do we change the school system? How do we replace the school system? How do we make a new school system? In recent years, this schools/school system focus has felt wrong to me, though for a while I did not understand why.

Now I know.

Our laser focus on schools and making them better has blinded us to what should be the real focus of our attention: *the people*. Good schools may make for better students, while they are in that school. But how sustaining is that for the individual student? Imagine a society in which we don't have to push or pull people to learn, but they clamor for it like teens waiting in line for the next video game release. Or, unlike what we have seen in New Orleans, student achievement is not driven by folks from the outside, but it happens because those within the given community passionately believe that education and learning is as important as the air we breathe. Unrealistic? I don't think so. I fervently believe that the next frontier for education is not education itself, but learning as a lifelong avocation. For that seemingly unlikely reality to exist, we need to become a learning culture.

It is now time to change the nature of the discussion. We need to change from an education culture which is focused on process, rules, systems, and politics to a learning culture focused on lifelong learning and the personal and national pride associated with that learning. This culture change needs to be built from the ground up, with the knowledge and understanding that our individual and collective learning is inextricably linked to our success. It's time for a pivot in the education conversation. It is time to build a national obsession around learning in America. We need to build a new learning culture in America.

11

Establishing a New Brand of Nationalism

In May 1961, President John F. Kennedy issued a challenge to Congress and to America. Making a direct link between tyranny and freedom, the president urged America to adopt the goal of landing a man on the moon by the end of the decade. In order for that to happen, the president reminded us that the country had to make a commitment beyond what it had made in the past. Implicit in his approach was the understanding that this was a national imperative, one that required unity of spirit. President Kennedy was asking that the collective will of America join together to achieve this noble goal. But he knew it wouldn't be easy. He said:

> I believe we possess all the resources and talents necessary. But the facts of the matter are that we have never made the national decisions or marshaled the national resources required for such leadership. We have never specified long-range goals on an urgent time schedule, or managed our resources and our time so as to insure their fulfillment.[1]

Kennedy's dramatic call to action ignited a level of American patriotism not seen in this country since World War II. For the rest of the 1960s, the space program was a national priority, a national obsession. The goal was clear: we were going to have an American walk on the moon and come home safely by the end of the decade. But for that to happen, every American had to do their part. In truth, he could have been talking about the state of education today.

In 2013, after using this example in a speech I gave in Alabama, a man approached me and agreed with me that this reference is dead-on correct. Apparently, his father worked for NASA in Houston. He related to me that when his family walked in restaurants, the other patrons would sometimes stand up and cheer. As he told me, "Everyone was invested in the space program. My dad was a celebrity because he was a scientist at NASA, but everyone felt like they were a part of the effort. If we could capture that same energy for education, it would be amazing."

Unfortunately, most Americans living today really don't know what that level of patriotism feels like. Over the last twenty years, the only event that has evoked nationalistic unity was the bombings of 9/11. Yes, we have had sporting events, like the Olympic Games and women's soccer that provide flashes of nationalism, but nothing has brought us together in a positive, sustained way that would contribute to the essence of our democracy, our country. A new energy around learning in America can be that catalyst.

Other countries are already engaged in a nationalist approach to education. Several years ago, as part of his landmark *ABC-TV* special," Stupid in America," John Stossel reported on how American schoolchildren were falling behind their counterparts in other nations. To make his point, he gave high schoolers at a highly regarded school in New Jersey the same test he had given to high schoolers at an average school in Belgium. The students in Belgium scored markedly higher on all the questions than did the students in New Jersey. Interestingly, the Belgium children acted like they were competing for the World Cup or some major political office. They talked about how their schools were better than ours and how excited they were to compete. And they called the American students stupid. Each Belgian student interviewed oozed confidence and national pride. Conversely, the New Jersey students were pretty nonchalant about the entire exercise. Yes, they were disappointed about the results, but, on balance, it did not seem to really affect them.[2]

All of us, particularly children like those in the story above, can benefit from a new nationalistic motivator in education. We need to give the term "Made in America" upgraded treatment and wrap national, education-related campaigns around that theme. Made in America should be designed to explain the relationship between learning and the new global dynamic we face in the future. Instead of asking children what they want to be when they grow up, we should adopt the approach used by my friend and Google's Education Evangelist Jaime Casap. When Jaime visits schools and talks with children (of all ages), he asks them, "What problem do you want to solve?" And, "Why?" Then he helps them understand the skills they will need to solve the problem they have identified. Jaime emphasizes that most of the jobs that elementary school children will have when they are adults don't exist today. And while we don't know what those jobs are, we do know that the needed skill sets begin with basic foundational proficiency. Geoffrey Canada, founder of Harlem's Children's Zone speaks often about the fact that by 2020, there will be 123 million skilled jobs available to be filled and today in the United States we are projected to have only fifty million residents with the skills needed to fill those jobs.[3]

Made in America should include everyone, even those remotely associated with education. But especially those directly involved in education. One group that has assiduously avoided getting involved in the K-12 discussion is the higher education community. In every state, there exists a host of well-respected universities and colleges. Yet, in most of those states, many of those same respected schools avoid getting mired in the K-12 issues in their backyards. Today, however, the crop of high-school graduates entering our colleges are not nearly as competent as they were in years past. This has led to more and more remedial classes in the basics: reading, reading comprehension, and math. The K-12 education shortfalls have also severely impacted the number of American high-school graduates qualified to major in math, science, and engineering in college.

Once when I was on a plane heading back to DC from a speech, the gentleman seated next to me started a conversation. Apparently, he recognized me and wanted to applaud me for my work. I was to find out that he was a university president from a major, well-known institution. He went on to tell me that at his university, less than 20 percent of his math, engineering, and science students were Americans. His graduate school numbers were worse in the same key areas. The students dominating the math, science, and engineering classes, he reported, were from India, China, and other Asian countries. He applauded the science, technology, engineering, and math (STEM) push by the federal government and the business community, but he also surmised that much of the effort may be too late. "We are so very far behind," he kept saying.

He then began to rail against the overall K-12 product he was getting from the schools in his state. Beyond the STEM needs, he insisted that too many of the children were just not college-ready. He decried the growing number of remedial courses he was forced to add to the freshman schedules. He said, "I can't tell you how many valedictorians and salutatorians I have seen in recent years who were forced to take remedial classes. That was unheard of years ago." While he did not say this directly, I sensed that he and his team are in an ongoing batter over admissions criteria and baseline university standards.

As I took all of this in, I could not help but begin to probe him about his relationship with the state's education superintendent and the various local superintendents from the assorted school districts in his state. At first, he shrugged my questions off, indicating that it didn't make sense for him to get involved in K-12 politics; that he had enough challenges with his budget. But as I pressed him by making the point that his growing remedial budget alone justified playing a more aggressive role in finding collaborative ways to press for change, he conceded the validity of my urgings. "I know we should get more involved," he said. "But when I speak with some of the local superintendents, I walk away feeling like they don't have a clue. So I just throw up my hands."

I am sure that many college presidents feel the same way about the local K-12 leadership in their respective states. This is where Made in America can make a difference. The STEM issue affects us all, and most college STEM enrollment numbers mirror those of my plane seat mate. Here, we can build college brands around STEM programs at local high schools that get these schools more visibly involved. Also, governors should convene both K-12 and higher education leaders together to find ways to elevate and celebrate joint efforts to grow learning. This national imperative should be planted in each and every state.

How do we brand learning as a national issue of patriotism? First, we must create a messaging framework that propels education to a top-of-mind issue for every parent, student, community member, and business owner. These stakeholders need to be able to know what they can do *now* to make a change. The contributions need to be able to scale—big companies can do big things, little children can do little things, and together we change it all.

Second, we must use imagery to help excite the possibilities of what our new learning culture looks like: a culture that acknowledges and cherishes all kinds of learning. American students must be made to feel as though their subject of interest matters, be it computer science, law, automotive services, music, business, plumbing, farming, or a host of other areas, it is all important. Ways must be developed to highlight these diverse learning areas with the overriding understanding that learning is not just important for going to college or getting a job; it is important for the on-going process of personal growth.

Third, we must engage the media to convince all stakeholders, but particularly students, that they own their future, they can drive change, and they have power. While the use of social media is key, so is using creative and new tools in traditional media to nurture our learning culture. How about a cable education channel or an education app tailored toward the messaging and images we know will suit our learning culture? At first glance, one might question how those tools would fit or even how we could keep the necessary content fresh. But those were the same questions the founders of ESPN faced when debating on whether to start a twenty-four-hour sports channel. Our vision should not be limited by what we now know. Instead, we must push for what we know we need as a learning community and let things organically grow and evolve.

Fourth, with everything that we do, our national focus must be uplifting, a message of unity. Through sports, music, and civics, we can use a variety of American themes to build unity around our learning culture. But we need not use this nationalist approach negatively. Our goal is to establish a national identity that places a renewed value and pride on learning—a new definition for Made in America.

Finally, we will know we are successful when

- We have established an identity we all want to own and actively participate in making possible.
- We all know why we are learning and that learning is a lifelong pursuit.
- The American public—everyone—knows that they are part of the change.
- We have national pride in all of our diverse learning modalities.
- Individuals leading the charge in developing varied sources of learning feel valued and part of our national learning community.

Notes

1. President John F. Kennedy, "NASA—Excerpt from the 'Special Message to the Congress on Urgent National Needs,'" delivered in-person before a joint session of Congress, May 25, 1961, NASA Website, accessed January 2, 2016, https://www.nasa.gov/vision/space/features/jfk_speech_text.html#.VoSI5pMrJ8c.
2. John Stossel, "John Stossel's 'Stupid in America,'" *ABC News* Online, January 13, 2006, http://abcnews.go.com/2020/Stossel/story?id=1500338.
3. Geoffrey Canada, *Foreword: Voices of Determination* by Kevin P. Chavous (New Brunswick: Transaction Publishers, 2012).

12

Removing Politics

Although politics is in the DNA of our democracy and politics has been the dominant driver of education policy throughout our history, we must do all we can to depoliticize learning in America. Its toxicity has made it increasingly difficult for student-centric approaches to take hold. Today, the shape of education policy is too dependent on which party is in charge or how compromise must take place to get the support for education policy that makes sense. Don't get me wrong; I am not naive and I totally understand the give and take of politics. But the day-to-day politics of education, state by state, is virtually killing our children's future. In addition to some of the stories I have shared regarding my own battles grappling over the politics of education, two other amazing examples illustrate this point.

In 2005, I was in South Carolina working with a group of national allies trying to get the governor and members of the state legislature to consider upgrading their charter school law and enact a statewide scholarship program to allow low-income children to go to private schools with public dollars. As I made my rounds, I was invited to speak with members of the South Carolina Black Caucus in a closed door meeting. With about fifteen members present, I began to talk about the successes we have had in DC with both charter schools and the DCOSP. I received a lot of probing questions, which I was able to handle well. At that point, in a moment of frustration, one member stood up and said, "Councilman, everything you have just said may be true. I will take your word for it. And, if we enact some of the laws you are suggesting, it may help some of our children. But I can't support any of it, even if it would help our children, because those Republicans are pushing it—the same ones who were fighting integration."

In response, I said, "While I appreciate the problem you have with many of those Republicans, which of course I share, there is no way I would vote against anything that will help our children learn."

Similarly, in 2013, I visited Alaska as its legislature was considering a statewide scholarship bill. As I was standing in the hall near the legislative chamber in Juneau, talking with the lead Republican sponsor of the bill, a Democrat walked by and stopped to chat with us. This particular Democrat was considering supporting the bill. Soon, as the three of us were talking, four or five other Republicans passed us by, a couple kind of stared at us, but they all kept walking. Later, the Republican bill sponsor said to me, "Boy, I am going to get in trouble with my Republican caucus because they saw me talking in the hall with some Democrats."

Moreover, on the twenty-fifth anniversary of *A Nation at Risk* report, the bipartisan group *Strong American Schools* said the reason why most of the report's thirty-eight recommendations haven't been adopted is simple: politics. Specifically, these words can be found in their report:

> While the national conversation about education would never be the same, stunningly few of the Commission's recommendations actually have been enacted. Now is not the time for more educational research or reports or commissions. We have enough common-sense ideas, backed by decades of research, to significantly improve American schools. The missing ingredient isn't even educational at all. It's political. Too often, state and local leaders have tried to enact reforms of the kind recommended in *A Nation at Risk* only to be stymied by organized special interests and political inertia. Without vigorous national leadership to improve education, states and local school systems simply cannot overcome the obstacles to making the big changes necessary to significantly improve our nation's K-12 schools.[1]

The politics of education has been the single biggest barrier to substantive change in education. The politics of education is killing our children.

On a national level, the partisanship on every major policy issue in America has infected our education policy-making with poisonous results. In 2013, former Clinton press secretary Mike McCurry gave a keynote address at the annual educational choice summit hosted by the American Federation for Children (AFC). McCurry bemoaned the current brazen partisanship driving policy, arguing that none of it is good for America and that, without a change, more political gridlock is inevitable. He pointed out that in 1982, there were 344 party switchers in Congress, members who would regularly cross party lines to vote for a proposal that made sense. In 2013, that number was down to thirteen members, meaning that nearly everyone in Congress votes totally in line with their political party. McCurry views educational choice as a way to take the partisanship out of politics and get our leaders to act with more aspiration and less parochialism. I agree.[2]

Let's look at the DCOSP as an example. Although I had to fight the Obama administration to keep the program alive, guess who are champions for the program in the Congress? Diane Feinstein, Rand Paul, Speaker John Boehner, and Cory Booker. It would be hard to find any other issue in which those four would agree to support.

But that support sure didn't matter to Eric Holder the night he verbally accosted me at the Kennedy Center. Looking back, I understand that he was in the throes of the day-to-day political gamesmanship all presidents and their team has to endure. And Eric Holder is a terrific guy, who I know cares about our children. At some point, however, our top leaders, especially our president, must start to separate education and learning from pedestrian politics.

Leadership does matter. In that regard, one of the best ways to get the politics out of education is for our political leaders to show leadership in doing so. In 2012, before the presidential debates between President Obama and Mitt Romney, I suggested that they show a new, forward-looking kind of leadership by agreeing not to debate education issues, but rather agree to sit down together in a bipartisan way to build a unified policy that really puts children first.

As I have traveled around the country, visiting schools, talking with teachers, parents, students, and elected officials, I am often asked why I take the stand that I take. In fact, it is not unusual for me to be pulled aside by elected officials so I can privately be told how much they support what I am saying and doing, but they can't publicly say what I say because they would get killed politically. I then invariably share parts of my story, my evolution as I began to get involved in reshaping education in DC. I tell them that each time I spoke with a different stakeholder in the education world, I got a different perspective, a different point of view. More often than not, those views centered around warring adult interests. At some point, I decided that I was going to divorce myself from myself as it relates to the politics of education. I had decided that each and every decision I would make regarding education or education policy would be based on one simple variable: Will this help a child learn? If the answer was yes, I would support it. If the answer was no, I would oppose it. Period. The purity of that approach is that it reduces every education question and proposal to its most basic form: the needs of our children. So what do I mean by the question, will it help a child learn? To be clear, I am not referring to curriculum, teaching styles, or teaching methodology. I am talking about the learning environment for children. I enthusiastically support and will fight for any learning environment that works for any child. And, in my view, that support is not tied to a system or certain type of education service delivery approach. It does not matter if it is a traditional public school, public charter school, private school, religious school, magnet school, specialty school, or virtual, digital, or blended learning school. It does not matter if the learning environment is a one-room schoolhouse with children of varying ages or a shed in someone's backyard or in the corner of a parking lot. If the environment is working for children or a child and they are learning, I support it—by any means necessary.

I can honestly say that there are several state legislators around the country who have changed their views and now speak out more forcefully in favor of school choice and parent empowerment after hearing me tell them about my approach. As much as possible, we need to elevate the thinking of our leaders. They are so used to being mired in the day-to-day political muck that it is hard for them to extend beyond themselves. We need a unified and consistent message of a higher calling—a higher goal centered around our children and our future—to change the priorities and focus of our leadership. Eventually, as the people become more emboldened with the possibilities associated with our new emphasis on learning, we can lead the leaders. There is no room for politics in our learning culture of tomorrow.

Notes

1. "A Stagnant Nation: Why American Students Are Still at Risk," ED in '08, April 2008, The Eli and Edythe Broad Foundation, accessed January 2, 2016, http://www.broadeducation.org/asset/1128-a%20stagnant%20nation.pdf.
2. "AFC Policy Summit—Mike McCurry," posted by American Federation for Children on May 21, 2013, https://www.youtube.com/watch?v=MnU-aIMexGxc&feature=youtu.be&noredirect=1.

13

All Children Can Learn

A key starting point to taking the steps needed to build a new learning culture in America is to believe that all children can learn, even if they are born in poverty. That being said, as we struggle with what ails many of our schools, more and more emphasis is being placed on the linkage between poverty and education, and the fact that poverty needs to be taken into account when we delve into issues pertaining to teacher effectiveness and the quality of a school's overall performance.

I get all that. And I do agree that there must be better coordination of services between schools and the entities that help families in poverty. I also acknowledge the impact of poverty on brain development and a child's ability to learn. Recent research from experts like Tammy Pawloski suggests that even under those circumstances, the brain can be healed and learning can take place. Dr. Pawloski is the director of the Center of Excellence to Prepare Teachers of Children of Poverty at Francis Marion University's Center for Excellence, and her work demonstrates that schools can create a culture of success for impoverished students.[1] But this discussion of the link between poverty and education extends beyond the medical research on the subject. Lurking beneath the surface often lies a veiled suggestion that some children can't learn—particularly children in poverty. That line of thinking is just plain wrong. Again, there are no winners and losers in a true learning culture because everyone learns, and everyone is a winner.

Throughout the history of our country, the unifying promise of America has been the hope for a better life for one's children through education, especially those children trapped in poverty. At every turn in our history, children in poverty have demonstrated their ability to learn and succeed.

During slavery, under some of the worst conditions known to man, some slaves taught their children to read by candlelight under the threat of death. Others were taught by benevolent whites, who risked prosecution for violating the laws that made it a crime to teach slaves to read. Even under those circumstances, those children learned—slaves like Olaudah Equiano, who wrote the first published book written by a slave, *The Interesting Narrative of the Life of Olaudah Equiano or Gustavus Vassa, the African.* Written in 1789, this remarkable book graphically chronicles Equiano's journey from his African village in Eboe (now, Nigeria), when he was stolen from his family at age eleven, to his ultimate freedom from slavery. Soon thereafter, he became a well-known abolitionist and activist against slavery and its horrors. Initially, after his capture Equiano was sold as a slave in Virginia. He graphically writes about how cruelly domestic slaves in Virginia were treated. They suffered punishments such as the "iron muzzle," which was used to keep house slaves quiet, leaving them unable to speak or eat. Much of Equiano's time in slavery, however, was spent serving the captains of slave ships and British navy vessels. One of his masters, Henry Pascal, the captain of a British trading vessel, gave Equiano the name Gustavus Vassa. Equiano served Pascal on several voyages across the Atlantic Ocean. As his time with Pascal progressed, Equiano professed a growing attachment to his master and a desire to imitate him and the English culture in which he was immersed. Before long, Equiano could speak English, but longed to learn how to read and write. During stopovers in England, Pascal sent Equiano to wait upon two white sisters known as the Miss Guerins. They became, in a sense, patrons to Equiano, not only treating him kindly but also supporting his education and his interest in Christianity by sending him to school. The Guerins were also instrumental in persuading Pascal to allow Equiano to be baptized into the church. Equiano was forever grateful to the two sisters, who "often used to teach me to read, and took great pains to instruct me in the principles of religion, and the knowledge of God. I therefore parted from those amiable ladies with reluctance; after receiving from them many friendly cautions how to conduct myself, and some valuable presents."[2] Once he eventually purchased his freedom from his final owner, Robert Kind, the reading and writing skills he obtained through those patron sisters gave him a platform to be an advocate for change. Those two sisters obviously helped Equiano believe in himself despite his indentured servitude.

Two hundred years later in California, folks like Cesar Chavez fought for better working conditions for Latino migrant workers. While those families struggled to make ends meet, many strived to put their children in schools that would meet their needs. And many of those children learned—children like Mari Carmen Lopez, who is featured in the book *Voices from the Fields: Children of Migrant Farmworkers Tell Their Stories*. At the time the book was published, Mari had graduated from high school and was preparing to attend California State University at Fresno, both firsts for her family. Here, Mari shares her story in her own words:

> I moved to the United States three years ago, when I was fifteen. Until then, I lived in Mexico City with my grandmother and my eight aunts and uncles. When I was a baby, my grandfather, mother, and father moved to America without me because the work opportunities were better. When I was very little, my mother sent my younger sister Jessica, soon after she was born in the U.S., to be with me in Mexico. My mother did that so I would have part of my family with me. I know it was hard for her.
>
> My mother waited until she was a United States citizen to bring me here. She and my father gave me a choice to stay in Mexico or come here. Even though I didn't want to leave my relatives there, I told them that I wanted to come to the U.S. to study. I wanted to be here with my parents, Jessica, and my youngest sister, Ariana. I wanted to learn English because I've always been told that with two languages one can be more prepared. I think that it was a good idea to come here and learn, but I miss my grandmother and her animo (encouragement). That is how she and my mother are alike. They always want the best for us. They say to keep on fighting and fighting, until we get the best.
>
> So now I live with my family in Chualar, California, on the property of a lettuce grower. Their lettuce fields are all around us, and my parents work very hard in them. On the weekends, I get up early and work in the fields. Usually I work in the furrows separating the lettuce plants. When I work with a hoe, my back gets sore and it can be a long and very hot day.
>
> My parents feel bad about working in the fields, but they don't have the education to be able to work in anything else. But education is very important them. They always tell us that we need to go

on studying so we don't have to work in the fields. One thing that working in the fields helped me understand is that it is not an easy life and that if you don't study, you'll have to work there. I learned that I need to keep moving forward if I don't want to pass my whole life working in the fields.

[. . .]

I was very, very nervous my first day at school. I took all my classes in Spanish, except for my class with my ESL (English as a Second Language) teacher. When I finished the first half of the year, I passed to taking my classes in English. My ESL teacher told us that there was an after-school program called SCORE that helped students with what they didn't understand in their homework. It was taught by migrant students who had high grades, and I thought that it was a good idea, since I didn't understand English or the homework for my classes. I didn't know anybody, but I went because my teacher told me about it.

[. . .]

Ever since we were little, I felt that my parents supported and encouraged us, and not everybody's do. For example, last year this boy I know dropped out of school to work in the fields with his father. My parents always help me, and I think what that boy needed was the encouragement of his parents to stay in school and their confidence in him, so that they all could see he could succeed. My mother has confidence in us and is very involved in the school. She's the vice president of the Migrant Parents Board and has always had close ties with my school.

Also, most of my teachers encouraged me to keep studying so I'll be able to help my parents and have a better future. Really there are many ways in which they can help us. If a student really wants to succeed, they can. Like when my ESL teacher gave me the idea to go to Yo Puedo. Yo Puedo means "I Can" in English, and it's a program for migrant farmworkers' children. It takes place in the summer at the campus of the University of California at Santa Cruz. When my teacher saw my grades, she said, "You qualify to go to YoPuedo. . ."

I wouldn't have been able to go to college if I hadn't gone to Yo Puedo. In the program, I studied drama, computers, ceramics, and literature written mostly by Mexicans, some who were migrant workers. We lived in dormitories at UCSC and it was very beautiful because we all lived together. Slowly, we all got to know each other, and we became like a family. My favorite class in Yo Puedo was drama because we could express in plays what was going on in real life, like school, or the community, or discrimination. They were like a force. They gave us power. They taught us to take risks and to rely on each other. We learned to always support each other and to say to each other, "Tu puedes, tu puedes." (You can, you can.) So going to Yo Puedo was my first risk and going to Fresno State is the next.[3]

Mari ended up in college because her parents and her ESL teacher believed in her—and she responded.

Following the Vietnam War, hundreds of thousands of Vietnamese refugees came to our nation. The vast majority of those children came to America unable to speak English and often lived with several families under one roof. Commonly referred to as the boat people, the Vietnamese immigrant education experience has proven to be rich and successful, in spite of their poor immigrant status. Countless studies reveal that Vietnamese immigrant families build their own learning culture for their children inside their homes.[4] This culture is wrapped around opportunity, hope, and the feeling that they must make sure that their children take advantage of being in the United States by getting as much education as possible. These parents feel an enormous sense of gratitude for being able to come to America and, as a result, they believe that the best way to honor their good fortune is through both hard work and their children's education. In *The Boat People and Achievement in America: A Study of Economic and Educational Success,* by Nathan Caplan, Marcella H. Choy, and John K. Whitmore, the authors use interviews and extensive surveys to analyze the noteworthy economic and educational success of Southeast Asian immigrants living in the United States. Their findings revealed that the immigrants' core values—namely, a cohesive family, hard work, and a commitment to education and achievement—helped them transcend their environment. In other words, these immigrants' cultural belief in education was so ingrained that it could not be altered by external factors. As far as the Vietnamese immigrant is concerned, poverty is in no way a barrier to learning. Indeed, they believe that if their children work hard enough, they can gain as much education as they want. In the book the authors quote one immigrant as saying, "I always remind my children that good education always helps one to get a good career, high position, better life. This country has many opportunities to get a good education. The only requirement is your goodwill. You have to put in your own energy, your own time, and your own effort to get what you want to have."[5]

In extolling the cultural virtues of the Vietnamese immigrants, the authors also lift up the promise and potential of public education, despite its frailties. But even they conclude that our approach must change—that learning must become more of a centerpiece in our culture.

> The schools cannot teach values by rote memory and expect them to produce the kinds of impact on learning reported in this study. They could be no more successful in that regard than they could be in force feeding formulas and facts to develop a taste for learning. What is essential to the transmission of the values that give priority to education is their early and deliberate promulgation by the adults in the family. We have probably gone too far, however, in the direction of believing that low-SES, single parent homes with large numbers of children cannot succeed in school. The critical issue is not the number and relationship of the adults in the household to the children but rather what dominates and who determines the nature and character of the milieu, its beliefs and behaviors. It means that the values and aspirations linked to student learning have to be instilled early and that an environment promotive of learning must be supported by families in a society concerned with the well-being of all of its members.[6]

The authors of *The Boat People and Achievement in America* understood the value of the learning culture they found among the boat people they studied. But they also appreciated, even when the book was published in 1989, that education in America can only work if a learning culture is established in our society.

For several generations, some of the consistently poorest Americans have been poor white children in places like Appalachia and the Mississippi Delta. Poverty in those places is further complicated by the inherent isolation found in rural settings. Yet despite theses challenges, some of those children learned. But they needed someone to believe in them. In Cynthia M. Duncan's book, *Worlds Apart: Why Poverty Persists in Rural America*, she examines the persistent patterns of poverty in places like the Appalachia mountain area of the eastern United States and the Mississippi Delta, which she renames Blackwell and Dahlia to protect the identity of those she interviewed. Professor Duncan conducted over 350 of those interviews and found an ingrained inequality that had eroded the fabric of the community and kept the residents she met in a consistent ongoing cycle of poverty, generation after generation. Those that were able to break away from this cycle were able to do so because of education. And because an adult close to them gave them the confidence to pursue their education. One such Appalachian-born woman interviewed was Joanne Martin. The oldest of eight children, Joanne spent most of her early youth helping to raise her younger siblings while her father spent years in and out of jail and her mother struggled to support the family. She stated that her dad likely had no higher than a first grade education, while her mother's education was likely no higher than fifth grade. At twelve, Joanne was sent away to a boarding school, a decision that "took all her mother's determination and the encouragement of a teacher who knew the family."

"My mother valued education," Joanne remembers, "even though she didn't have any formal education herself. But the high school that I would have had to go to was like twenty miles from home and they didn't run a bus, due to the county politics at that time. . . I don't think it was a big decision for my mother. . . but a grade school teacher who was our next-door neighbor had attended that boarding school, and she helped my mother understand what school was about, and the importance of my going. She played a really big role."

The opportunity changed Joanne's life forever. "To me, it was an excellent experience," Joanne said. "I really hate that those boarding schools are no longer available because I think they were more instrumental in more people going to college and to high school than anything else. It removed you from the only environment you've ever known. I had never been more than twenty miles from my home until then. If you grow up with everybody being the same, you don't know that there is another way of life or another goal, or anything to aim for."[7]

Joanne graduated from college, became a healthcare administrator, and broke the cycle of poverty in her own family—because of a neighbor who believed in her.

Not surprisingly, at the end of her book, Professor Duncan writes about the importance of education in breaking the cycle of poverty in America. She notes that everyone she interviewed in Appalachia or the Delta who "made it" finished school, and that as a result of that education, all of them left poverty behind. The problem, she notes, is that America's poor communities do not give their residents an equal opportunity to get a quality education.

"One thing that makes establishing good schools a viable policy idea, even as we enter the twenty-first century, is that doing so does not require a complete turnabout in American social policy," Professor Duncan writes. "And the idea that every American child is entitled to a good public education is a well-established part of American ideology. Local control over education is, of course, also a strongly held tenet, and it is clear that creating good schools to serve poor children would require challenging local control, at least in poor places like Blackwell and Dahlia. Our allegiance to the principle of local control in these places, as the inner-city schools described by Jonathan Kozol, Alex Kotlowitz, William Julius Wilson, and others, protects bad practices and absolves us all of responsibility to provide equal opportunity for all American children. The system cries out for change."

What Professor Duncan is alluding to is the dual system of expectations placed on the children of the haves versus the children of the have-nots. All children can learn—even our poor children. Interestingly, in looking at the income achievement gap, McKinsey & Company came to the same conclusion. The report noted:

> The wide variation in performance among schools serving similar students suggests that these gaps can be closed. Race and poverty are not destiny.[8]

Frankly, some of the growing articles and studies on this topic oftentimes engage in excuse-making and justify the "throwing up of the hands" as it relates to trying to teach children in poverty.

Remember the teacher who told me she was doing the best she could to help those ghetto children? Unfortunately, that way of thinking is more prevalent than we realize. Even among the education reform community, there are those who really don't believe that all children can learn.

I discussed this issue with a terrific school leader in St. Louis who bemoaned the fact that far too many people blatantly share with her thoughts like "it's impossible to educate poor black children" and "you need to change your school's demographic to have any real success."

What's worse is that far too many adults who are in positions of influence and authority around children convey that belief directly to the children, both verbally and nonverbally. To this day, I want to blame my second teacher for my hating math. It may not be fair and because of the family support I had, it may not be accurate, but it certainly applies in many classrooms in subpar schools located in challenged neighborhoods. All children can learn. But all children cannot learn in the same way. It is incumbent upon us to meet these children where they are and utilize the approach that best serves them, including offering more quality options for them. Teachers are the single biggest factor in a child's education. There are many teachers who have worked their magic with children who come from the most challenged environments imaginable. As was recommended in *A Nation at Risk*, we must commit to professionalizing our teaching corp and having the very best teachers in our most troubled schools, teachers who believe all children have value and all children can learn. We cannot be a nation of learners if our educators do not believe that the children they serve can learn.

Then it is essential that we instill in our children the belief that they can learn. They need to *feel* that belief. Often, a little bit goes a long way. If we prod them, encourage them, support them, inspire them, and motivate them, our children will respond. Just like Helen Shelton encouraged, inspired, and motivated me.

Fun is another great motivational tool. One of the reasons why technology, video games, and computers appeal to children of all ages is that they are fun. Fun matters. Somehow, in our zeal to get more out of our children educationally, it seems we have forgotten how important it is to making learning fun. What's more, Made in America should take advantage of experiential and virtual learning to make sure that children's learning is fun. The problem with the drill and kill over allegiance to testing is that it takes the fun out of learning. Each child's educational experience should have a balance of learning activities to ensure that each child is acquiring information and enjoying it at the same time. Made in America should enhance a child's natural curiosity, not destroy it.

No one understands this more than Dr. Sugata Mitra. Dr. Mitra is a renowned professor of education technology, a physicist, and scientist by profession. He also has a passion for computer-based education. He believes that children, even those in poverty, can educate themselves provided that they have access to a computer and the Internet. Dr. Mitra is now best known for his famous *TED Talk* in which he described his "hole in the wall" experiment. Widely studied and cited, Dr. Mitra's hole in the wall experiment reminds us of how powerful curiosity is in a child's learning experience.[9]

In order to test his theories about children' ability to teach themselves on the Internet, Dr. Mitra launched his hole in the wall experiment by imbedding a fully Internet-connected PC into a concrete wall in a poor area south of New Delhi, India. To westerners, it would look like an ATM machine, but none of the people in this poor village had ever seen anything like it. Dr. Mitra installed the computer, turned it on, and left, thereby allowing any passerby to play with it. He monitored the activity in the PC using a remote computer and a video camera mounted on a nearby tree.

What he discovered was that the most avid users of the machine were ghetto children aged six to twelve, most of whom have only the most rudimentary education and little, if any, knowledge of English. Yet, within days, the children had taught themselves to draw on the computer and to browse the Internet. The children also learned a host of other things, including enough workable English, so they could competently surf the net. For the next ten years, Dr. Mitra repeated his experiment in areas even more remote than that original New Delhi slum. Later, he included a Skype component so that the children could communicate with an older lady who would read to them and share stories with them. This "grandmother" type became a fixture in his experiments.

Dr. Mitra remains astonished by what these children were able to learn on their own. During one experiment, he created the hole in the wall, asked the children to solve a complicated physics problem, and left. The children were all very young and none of them had ever been exposed to physics. Nor did they know English. When he came back days later, the children looked sullen. Dr. Mitra assumed they were upset because they could not solve the problem. In actuality, the children did have the answer; they had just assumed that there was more than one answer and were disappointed that they couldn't discover anything beyond the first.[10]

Dr. Mitra believes that today's technology, coupled with a child's natural inquisitiveness, could almost make teachers obsolete. Pretty radical. But, it is clear that our current system, known to snuff the curiosity out of children who "don't fit in" is not the system of the future.

I had a chance to speak with Dr. Mitra in 2014, after he gave the keynote at the American Federation for Children Summit in Orlando. As a result of his years working with the hole in the wall experiment, he insightfully believes that folks are wrong when they keep talking about our education system being broken. He says, "it's quite fashionable to say that the education system's broken—it's not broken, it's wonderfully constructed. It's just that we don't need it anymore. It's outdated." If anything, his experiment with those children in underdeveloped villages around the world proves just that.

As it relates to education in America, it is time for us to aggressively use those same tools—technology and exciting the natural curiosity of children—to help shape a new culture of learning, one that suits our evolution as a society. The proper starting point is to transform America into a community of learners.

By allowing students to learn by experience and making learning fun, Dr. Mitra has created a culture of learning.

Once we truly embrace and believe that all children can learn, we can then build our new learning culture in America. As has been outlined previously, we must build a new brand of patriotism around learning, a brand of nationalism that rises above politics. But keep in mind that unlike each and every attempt to reform education, building a new American learning culture takes the focus away from schools and the education system and places it on individuals. Our goal is to inspire every American to want to learn so that we can build a true community of learners.

Notes

1. For information on the research that has come out of Francis Marion Center for Excellence, please see these resources,
    – An article on Tammy Pawloski and how her research has aided schools: Elizabeth Lamb, "Pawloski Creates 'Culture of Success' for Impoverished Students," SC Now Morning News Online, December 17, 2011, http://www.scnow.com/news/local/article_334df023-56c8-54fc-b302-a805c57eecba.html.
    – Studies that support the claim that poverty has a negative impact on brain development and size: Joan Luby, et al., "The Effects of Poverty on Childhood Brain Development: The Mediating Effect of Caregiving and Stressful Life Events," *JAMA Pediatrics*167, no. 12 (2013): 1135–1142. doi:10.1001/jamapediatrics.2013.3139. http://archpedi.jamanetwork.com/

article.aspx?articleid=1761544. And Richard Monastersky, "Researchers Gain Understanding of How Poverty Alters the Brain," *The Chronicle of Higher Education*, February 18, 2008, http://chronicle.com/article/Researchers-Gain-Understand/516/.

– Studies that support the claim that the negative impacts of poverty can be mediated by good education and mentorship: Elisabeth D. Babcock, "Using Brain Science to Design New Pathways Out of Poverty," Crittenton Women's Union, 2014, http://www.liveworkthrive.org/site/assets/Using%20Brain%20Science%20to%20Create%20Pathways%20Out%20of%20Poverty%20FINAL%20online.pdf. And Elisabeth D. Babcock, "Rethinking Poverty," Stanford Social Innovation Review, Fall 2014, http://www.liveworkthrive.org/site/assets/docs/SSIR_Fall_2014_Rethinking_Poverty.pdf.

2. Olaudah Equiano, *The Interesting Narrative of the Life of Olaudah Equiano, or Gustavus Vassa, the African* (London, 1794), 9th ed.enlarged, 88.

3. S. Beth Atkin, *Voices from the Fields: Children of Migrant Farmworkers Tell Their Stories* (Boston, MA: Little, Brown and Company, 1993), 87–91.

4. "Vietnamese Americans," Pew Research Center: Social & Demographic Trends, accessed January 2, 2016, http://www.pewsocialtrends.org/asianamericans-graphics/vietnamese/.

5. Nathan Caplan, John K. Whitmore, and Marcella H. Choy, *The Boat People and Achievement in America: A Study of Economic and Educational Success* (Ann Arbor: The University of Michigan Press, 1989), 127.

6. Nathan Caplan, John K Whitmore, and Marcella H. Choy, *The Boat People and Achievement in America: A Study of Economic and Educational Success* (Ann Arbor: The University of Michigan Press, 1989), 176.

7. Cynthia M. Duncan, *Worlds Apart: Why Poverty Persists in Rural America* (New Haven, CT: Yale University Press, 1999), 59–60.

8. "The Economic Impact of the Achievement Gap in America's Schools," McKinsey & Company: Social Sector Office, April 2009, http://mckinseyonsociety.com/downloads/reports/Education/achievement_gap_report.pdf, 6.

9. Sugata Mitra, "Kids Can Teach Themselves," LIFT 2007, TEDTalks filmed April 2007, accessed January 2, 2016, https://www.ted.com/talks/sugata_mitra_shows_how_kids_teach_themselves.

10. Sugata Mitra and Vivek Rana, "Children and the Internet: Experiments with Minimally Invasive Education in India," *British Journal of Educational Technology* 32, no. 2 (2001): 221–32, http://hole-in-the-wall.com/docs/paper02.pdf.

14

Encouraging Education Activism

When looking at how education is changing and the factors contributing to positive changes, it is important to look at children who want to learn and who have stories that inspire learning. The most well known of these voices is the Nobel Peace Prize winning teenager, Malala Yousafzai. Malala is an eighteen-year-old Pakistani girl who, at age eleven, defied the Taliban by declaring that she was going to go to school. Under the Taliban's extremist Muslim views, women are not allowed to be educated, have professional jobs, or dress in a manner in which too much of their skin is visible. With bold and brash style, young Malala began championing education for Muslim women through a blog on the British Broadcasting Company. At one point she said, "I don't mind if I have to sit on the floor at school. All I want is an education. And I'm afraid of no one." Such brazen and insolent behavior from everyday citizens is unheard of in that part of the world, especially from a little girl. Soon after she started her blog, the Taliban threatened to put Malala in her place. True to their word, in 2012, a Taliban hit squad shot Malala while she was on the bus headed to school. Malala was fourteen years old. Also shot in the shoulder and hand was Malala's best friend, Shazia Razman, who was sitting next to Malala on the school bus. Incredibly, Malala fully recovered from the shooting. And despite the Taliban's threats, Yousafzai remains a staunch advocate for the power of education.

In 2014, at age seventeen, Malala became the youngest Nobel Peace Prize laureate ever.[1] She also has helped start a school for girls in Syria and has challenged world leaders to stop war and support education through her #BooksNotBullets campaign. Though young, Malala's vision is entirely consistent with the type of learning culture we need in America. Her message centers around the priority—or lack thereof—governments place on giving all of their people the education that they deserve. And her resiliency reminds us that so many of our children want to learn and will fight for their education.

I decided to write my last book, *Voices of Determination: Children That Defy the Odds*, because I was becoming more and more amazed by the incredible stories of resiliency and determination in many of the children that I met. In the book, I feature ten children who overcame incredible odds just to get their education. These children, and their steadfast desire to learn, represent the best examples of what a learning culture should be. Some of the children endured incest, homelessness, drug and alcohol addiction, and gang activity, but each survived and ultimately thrived. Working on the book also solidified my view that we needed a new learning culture in America. The stories I share are heart-wrenching and inspiring, just like the children who lived them: children such as Zina, another amazing young woman victimized by the Taliban's barbaric practices. Zina migrated to the states with her mother and siblings once the Taliban took over the country in the late 1990s. The Taliban killed her father and grandfather and took away her mother's college professorship. In fact, the Taliban instantly changed Afghanistan from a country with progressive views toward women to a country in which women were relegated to sexist policies from hundreds of years ago. All of the women in the country had to wear full-body burkas and none could go to school or work outside of the home.

By the time fourteen-year-old Zina arrived in the states with her mother and her siblings, she had not been in a classroom for six years and could not speak English. She landed in a traditional urban public school in which she received no instruction or help. In fact, since no one at the new school spoke Farsi, her native language, she was told by her teacher to just stay in her seat and follow as best she could. She was never tested, never graded, and never engaged. Eventually, she ended up in a charter school where the teachers went out of their way to help Zina learn. Through it all, her steadfast desire to be educated remained constant. Recently, Zina graduated from college and now works for the European Union helping oppressed women in her former country.[2]

After working on the book, I realized that Zina, the other children I profiled, and scores of others are already part of that new culture: they just don't know it: children like twelve-year-old Tyrell, who lives in Baton Rouge, Louisiana. For years, Tyrell went to a bad school and his grades suffered as a result. He hated school because his teachers did not care and some of the other more disruptive children had a free rein to wreck havoc. As extreme as this sounds, there are many schools that fit the same description. Fortunately for Tyrell, he received a scholarship to attend a private school from the Louisiana Scholarship Program. Almost instantly, Tyrell fell in love with his school. He couldn't wait to get up in the morning; he liked it so much. Soon after Tyrell started in his new school, the Louisiana teachers union filed a lawsuit in an effort to try to kill the program. On the day of the court hearing, Tyrell begged his mother to let him miss school so he could join the adults rallying in front of the courthouse to keep the program alive. Tyrell was the only child at the rally. Holding a sign that said "Put Children First," Tyrell told me why coming to the rally meant so much to him. "I had to come," he said. "When I heard I might lose my scholarship, I got scared at the thought that I might have to go back to my old school, which would be horrible. I've been worrying about this so much, I can't even sleep at night."[3]

Zina, Tyrell, and countless nameless children across America are living proof of the new learner, willing to fight to learn. These children can be the best examples we can use to inspire other children that they can too.

And how about those nine public school students who stepped up and sued the state of California in the case, *Vergara v. California*? Those children's fight stemmed from the basic belief that access to qualified teachers should be fair and widespread, that classroom safety is paramount, and that equity remains essential. In specifically attacking California's teacher tenure law, these students argued that it wasn't fair or equitable that California had a proven history of sending the worse teachers to the most challenged schools; that the last-in, first-out law wrongly gives priority to seniority over success in times of teacher layoffs; and that the consequences of bad teaching negatively follows these students the rest of their lives: not just in test scores, but in jobs and earning potential. The students won their case on all counts and the case is now on appeal, but lawsuits similar to *Vergara v. California* are popping up all over America. Children want to learn and they are tired of the staid, antiquated rules of the system getting in the way of their learning. The judges are beginning to listen to our children.[4]

Finally, what better champion for children can there be than parents? America opinion is conflicted when it comes to parents of school-age children. On the one hand, parents are asked to be more engaged in their children's learning, yet through tone and demeanor (which can often be outright hostile), many school administrators and teachers really don't want parents around much—unless it's within the well-defined box designed for them.

In visiting with parents around the country, I know one truism: parents want what's best for their children. More often than not, the average parent has wrapped their hopes, dreams, and aspirations around their children's future with the ultimate belief that their children's lives will be better than theirs. What a dynamic to build on. And yet, amazingly, we haven't done so. We generally give parents lip service, and as we engage in reform efforts around the country, the parent outreach component is usually an afterthought. What if we did the reverse? What if, in building this new nation of learners, all reform efforts began with parents and their children? When the end user is inspired, magic happens. Just ask Steve Jobs!

Just like the children I mentioned previously, there are numerous examples of parents fighting for their children's education, taking on the current intractable system and working wonders. And often, those parents become the conduit for greater learning among their fellow parents and neighbors. The expression "each one teach one" has special meaning when parents are enthusiastically engaged.

I have been privileged to have worked with some incredible parents from various parts of the country. Parents like Shree Medlock, BAEO's former national advocacy director. When Shree was BAEO's Louisiana state director, she helped to organize and train parents in New Orleans and around the state. When the Louisiana legislature passed a scholarship bill for low-income New Orleans children, Shree and her team began training parents on how to be advocates for their children. For many of these predominately low-income parents, the training was huge. Since most were uneducated and intimidated by the school system, they often found themselves stymied as to how to even speak with their children's teachers—even when they "felt" as though something was wrong. When Shree and her team were done with the training, even parents who were illiterate felt empowered enough to talk with teachers and school officials. They were even able to make sure their children were doing their homework.

More significantly, once these parents' children were enrolled in their new schools, the parents were surprised by how much the children loved them. Soon, many of these parents—feeding on the enthusiasm they witnessed in their children—began to revisit their own education. Several enrolled to take GED courses. Yes, the children were leading the parents.

Shree understood how helpless these parents felt. She was once in that position herself. Though highly educated, she was shocked to learn that her own son couldn't read. When she approached her son's teacher and the school leaders, they put the blame on Shree's son. After much back and forth, Shree was finally able to get her son in the right educational environment that worked for him. From that moment on, Shree became a steadfast advocate for educational choice.

Shree Medlock is not alone. Gwen Samuel has fought for parents rights through her Parent Revolution network in Connecticut; Virginia Walden Ford, the DC parent leader who helped drive grassroots support for the DCOSP, is now organizing parents in her home state of Arkansas; and parents like Ohio's Kelley Williams-Bolar and Pennsylvania's Hamlet Garcia have been prosecuted for using a relative's address to send their children to better schools. Kelley was jailed and ridiculed by a judge who said she was "stealing an education," even though the Akron school attended by Kelley's daughter was one of the worst schools in the state. At the time, I said that the judge should prosecute the Akron, Ohio, school district. Kelley's case made her a national cause célèbre.

And then there were the Latino parents in Compton, California, who were sick and tired of having to send their children to a terrible neighborhood school. They decided to use the newly enacted parent trigger law to get relief. This landmark legislation, authored by the inimitable legislator Gloria Romero, mandated that the school district had to replace a failing school's principal and staff or convert the school to a charter school if a majority of the parents in the school signed a petition demanding the change.[5] Once these parents submitted their petition, the school district fought them tooth and nail. They questioned the validity of the signatures; they challenged the parents' citizenship (totally irrelevant, since even children of illegal aliens are entitled to a free and appropriate education in the United States) and generally tried to intimidate them individually. After months and months of fighting, the parents ultimately won. A host of parent trigger bills have been introduced in legislatures around the country—just because those Latino parents had the courage to fight for their children.

Beyond the needed activism, there also exists any number of parents who are grateful to see their children learning in ways they never imagined. Parents like the Somali woman whose daughter attends a charter school in Utah. Salt Lake City has become a destination point for refugee children from all over the world. For a time, most of these families and their children were forced to go to a low-performing public school near the public housing project where they lived. Think about it. You bring children, who may be amputees or burn victims, to America, with the promise of a new life, then you place them in the projects and make them go to a bad school. Well, thanks to a benevolent businessman and his sister, a state-of-the-art charter school was founded right in that very neighborhood to educate those children. The results have been terrific. The children do extremely well on standardized tests and, more importantly, their spark for learning has been nurtured and expanded. The mother I spoke with was in tears reflecting on how this school has helped build her daughter's bright future.

I had a similar experience when I met with several parents at Harlem Success Academy Charter School in New York. Founded by Eva Moskowitz, Harlem Success is one of the highest performing schools in the state. During a conversation with one of the students' grandmothers, she shared with me that just about everyone in her family grew up in Harlem and subsequently experienced the hardships of growing up in poverty and ultimately attended failing schools: with one exception—her granddaughter—a student at Harlem Success.

She eloquently said: "Four generations of Harlem women and we finally have one who may make it to college." She shared with me that she is proud of the achievements of her granddaughter and that she sometimes finds herself wondering "what might have been" if she too had the opportunity to learn. But her heart was "overfilled with joy" knowing that her granddaughter had a future.

This grandmother, and many others before her, attended a predictably failing school. For a century and a half, there has been little substantive change in the way we educate our children. The classic approach in America's classrooms remains essentially a one-size-fits-all undertaking.

I have been fortunate to hear firsthand the poignant, inspiring stories of parents who graciously celebrate the learning experiences of their children. These positively infectious stories often serve to inspire the parents themselves to rethink their lives and pursue new learning opportunities they once thought had passed them by. Like their children, these "new" voices must be featured more by us as well. As more and more everyday citizens see living, breathing examples of folks like them who get inspired by learning, those same everyday citizens will become inspired to advance their own learning. The individual pride associated with that momentum helps to build the national pride we need to make education and learning our top priority.

These themes may sound challenging to some, untenable to others. But in various pockets throughout America they are being utilized, implemented, and embraced. There are an increasing number of citizens who are beginning to look at education much differently than they had been accustomed to. And all of them are Made in America. We must share their stories and amplify their voices as we build our new culture of learning. More than a new law or a new idea, we need a new energy and a new enthusiasm to drive our new culture of learning in America.

Notes

1. "Nobel Laureates by Age," The Official Website of the Novel Prize, accessed January 4, 2016, http://www.nobelprize.org/nobel_prizes/lists/age.html.
2. Kevin Chavous, *Voices of Determination: Children That Defy the Odds* (New Brunswick: Transaction Publishers, 2012), 45–64.
3. Kevin Chavous, "Using Lawsuits to Hurt Kids," Bean Soup Times, August 20, 2015, http://beansouptimes.com/using-lawsuits-to-hurt-kids/#sthash.zd2M8i7A.dpbs.

4. Lyndsey Layton, "California Court Rules Teacher Tenure Creates Impermissible Unequal Conditions," *The Washington Post* Online, June 10, 2014, https://www.washingtonpost.com/local/education/calif-court-rules-teacher-tenure-creates-unequal-conditions/2014/06/10/8be4f64a-f0be-11e3-914c-1fbd0614e2d4_story.html. For the case, please see Vergara v. California, No. BC484642 (Cal. Super. Ct. August 27, 2014), http://studentsmatter.org/wp-content/uploads/2014/08/SM_Final-Judgment_08.28.14.pdf. Decision has been appealed. Vergara v. California, No. B258589 (Cal. Ct. App.) (case pending).

5. Amanda Paulson, "Education Reform: California to Join Race to the Top Rush," The Christian Science Monitor Online, January 5, 2010, http://www.csmonitor.com/USA/Education/2010/0105/Education-reform-California-to-join-Race-to-the-Top-rush.

15

Considering How Other Cultures Teach and Learn

In 1999, I visited Taipei, Taiwan, as part of a delegation of DC Council members organized by Chairperson Linda Cropp. During our trip, we visited members of the country's legislature and judiciary and spent a fair amount of time with Taipei Mayor and future Taiwan President Ma Ying-jeou. Linda (a former DC school board president), Gwendolyn Orange (councilmember Vincent Orange's wife and a DC public schools teacher), and I had an interest in education, so we were able to arrange a separate visit to a school designed for children with special needs. None of us expected what we saw. And it started with the greeting we received when we entered that school at 8 AM on a Saturday morning.

As soon as we walked into the gym, a band started playing and the packed stands of several hundred people erupted. Once he got the cheers going, the school principal ran down from the stage to greet us. He gave Linda and Gwen flowers and greeted me with a bear hug. I turned to look at the crowd and the audience, which was still wildly cheering, looked back at me like I was Michael Jordan. After a few more minutes of sustained applause, the principal, a short, lean, exuberant man with a round, pleasant face, began to wave his arms up and down trying to quiet the crowd. But they wouldn't stop! The audience kept cheering until the principal started speaking into the microphone. Since I do not understand Mandarin Chinese, I couldn't know what he said, but he did mention each of our names, which led to more sustained applause. Then Linda spoke and our tour of the school, with our interpreter in tow, began.

The school was set up for children with mild mental retardation and cognitive deficits. It was the equivalent of a high school and in addition to mastering the needed academics, each student had to demonstrate an ability to, as the principal kept saying, "make it on their own without supervision." The principal then explained that the Taiwanese possess a core belief that all citizens have value; that each and every individual can contribute to the uplifting of their family and their country by being the best that they can be, irrespective of their aptitude or skill level. Therefore, he said, the government makes sure that they give each student the best education possible. Education issues were rarely subject to political debates. This was the same sentiment expressed to us in earlier visits with members of the country's legislature.

The principal also told us that there was no negative stigma attached to children who were a little different. This fact was obvious to Linda, Gwen, and me since we happened to see some mentally challenged cashiers at a McDonald's downtown. We were struck by how patient and encouraging the long line of customers were with those cashiers. We also noticed how nonchalant, yet caring the other school-age students treated them. We had no idea that the very next day, we would be visiting the school that likely educated those cashiers.

The principal then made it clear that the country's cultural belief that all citizens have value extends beyond the classroom. We learned that each student had a job waiting for them at a fast food restaurant or a grocery store once they graduated. In fact, the need to demonstrate that they could make it on their own without supervision meant that the students had to show that they could leave school on their own, catch a bus downtown, make it to their place of employment on time, then catch a bus home. During their last semester, every senior and their parents had to attend a life skills program on Saturday mornings where they learned how to navigate life beyond the cocoon of the school. On the Saturday we visited the school, nearly two hundred parents were sitting in various classrooms working with the school's staff on getting the children ready for the working world. Before we left, an awards ceremony took place in the gym where several students were honored for being able to leave the school, take the bus, make it to work on time, and then take the bus home, all without asking for help. As each student received their award, some were so happy that they began to cry, as the crowd cheered them on like rock stars. As we watched with amazement, Linda leaned over and said to me, "Wouldn't it be something if we valued our special needs children like this?"

Later, when I shared the experience with Mayor Ma, I probed him more about the politics of education. Mayor Ma had been educated in the United States, first at New York University and then at Harvard. He was well aware of the American politics in general and education politics specifically. He candidly said to me, "Councilman, unlike the States, we feel that the education of our children is too important of an issue for us to fight over. We do value each child and our people know that just by doing their part. Getting as much education as they can, it helps us all."

As was highlighted in the McKinsey report, the most obvious evidence of America's slippage in educational attainment can be seen when comparing the proficiency of American school-age children with the proficiency of school-age children from other industrialized nations around the world. The Program for International Student Assessment (PISA) has conducted international educational attainment rankings since 2000. PISA is an arm of the Organisation for Economic Co-operation and Development (OECD). The mission of OECD is to promote policies that will improve the economic and social well-being of people around the world. Their most recent survey—PISA's fifth—was in 2012. That survey assessed the competencies of fifteen-year-olds in reading, mathematics, and science (with a focus on mathematics) in sixty-five countries and economies.

Approximately 510,000 students between the ages of fifteen years three months and sixteen years two months participated in the survey, representing a total of around twenty-eight million fifteen-year-olds globally.[1]

Since the initial PISA rankings first came out in 2000, educators and policymakers have all been scratching their heads, trying to figure out how to stop our country's growing educational shortfalls. But they are just about the only Americans paying attention to those statistics. Most Americans don't even know what PISA is, nor could they care less. And that, too, is part of the problem.

For example, when the first PISA rankings were released in 2000, nearly every citizen in Germany went into a malaise. The Germans have always prided themselves on their intellect and their educational system. The country was universally shocked when they discovered that they were ranked below average on literacy and mathematics.[2] The PISA rankings were all over the news, discussed in offices, at parties, during sporting events. Teachers everywhere were embarrassed and students were depressed. The country was downright apoplectic about the results. As is the case with any national crisis, in any country, a series of emergency government meetings followed and the German people redoubled their efforts to work harder and do better—as a nation. It became a national imperative. The efforts Germany put in to improve its schooling are evident in their subsequent PISA rankings, as they are one of the few countries whose score has improved every year.[3] That's right: how German children performed in school became a national priority. Germany has a learning culture.

Taiwan, Germany, Finland, Belgium, Singapore, and other countries regularly outpace our children educationally. And that hasn't changed since PISA began tracking the educational outputs of the industrialized nations. Why not? Education reform efforts are underway in every US state; K-12 education funding is a large chunk of most state budgets; and education is viewed as a "top priority" to most Americans.[4] Yet, the United States has not improved on any measures since PISA's first survey in 2000.[5] If education truly is a top priority, what is it that is these other countries are doing that we are not?

For those of us engaged in this work, we have been struggling with those questions for years. But maybe we have been asking the wrong questions, dealing with the wrong assumptions, and responding to false premises. Maybe we have not dug deep enough as we formulate education policy. Maybe our collective image of education is so ingrained in our culture that we need to look at that culture to understand it, then change it.

As antiquated as it may seem, the following images are as American as apple pie: the red brick schoolhouse in the neighborhood; parents walking their children to school; 9 AM to 3 PM school day; periodic PTA meetings in the child's classroom; middle schoolers being able to get lockers and change classes; school science fairs; school dances; weekend athletic events; the prom; school graduation ceremonies; summer recess. As each of you read these words, powerful, nostalgic memories emerge. Even for me. At the beginning of this book, you read as I intimately described my first day of school! These images, and many others, are part of our American culture. They represent who we are and what we are as a country. They are ingrained images for all of us as to what education looks like. So when you think about it, it makes sense that some view aggressive reform efforts as a personal attack.

Remember when Chicago Mayor Rahm Emanuel caught all that heat for closing schools? Folks were outraged. And it did not matter that the schools targeted were just plain horrible. None of the children were learning in those schools. But if you paid attention to the interviews, you heard people refer to the schools as being "stabilizing forces in our community" and folks feeling like they were "being disrespected by the Mayor." The "community," as is the case throughout the country, is viewed as the physical neighborhood and its institutions, its structures, its people. For most Americans, there is no stronger institution than their church and their neighborhood school.

For the last twenty years, those of us pressing the system to change have been implicitly asking people to reject what they are comfortable with, to renounce what they know.

If we understand this phenomenon, we can then understand how and why other countries are better able to embrace creativity and innovation in education. Most other industrialized nations do not have the entrenched educational establishment that is so intertwined with their culture, which, in turn, gives them more freedom to rebuild, to accept the new. The culture that has been established in most other nations, however, is a culture of learning that extends far beyond formal education. As Taipei Mayor Ma reminded me, these other nations *value* each and every citizen and understand the need to *invest* in each of them. These nations understand that the process of learning extends beyond a school day or formal education. Learning should be viewed as a lifelong endeavor.

So, how do we rise above the Byzantine, political, and parochial issues embedded in American education to advance learning, to build a nation that celebrates learning? Well, to begin with, we must elevate the discussion and redefine what education really means. In celebrating each person's learning potential, we also help redefine "community," which will also include our community of learners.

By infusing a new mindset, a new energy, and a new culture into education, we "fix" the education problem in America and we create a national obsession around learning. An obsession centered on personal and national pride in learning and educational growth. In essence, our charge is to inspire America to take national and personal pride in learning.

This new culture will only emerge by shifting the focus of education reform away from the punitive and toward the positive. Instead of talking about failing schools and why we can't close the various achievement gaps in this country, we need to pivot: use a new national mindset to focus on models that work and excite the possibilities associated with twenty-first century customized leaning. We thereby make our citizens' education experience positively infectious, rather than the chore it has become in far too many school districts.

This new approach requires a concentrated strategy and focus. At every stage, our default mode should be to inspire and encourage. Sure, tough love will be needed from time to time, but to build a nation of learners, we must always appeal to our better selves and our internal desire to be better and do better.

Notes

1. "PISA 2012 Results," The Organisation for Economic Co-operation and Development (OECD) Official Website, accessed January 2, 2016, http://www.oecd.org/pisa/keyfindings/pisa-2012-results.htm.
2. "Germany: Once Weak International Standing Prompts Strong Nationwide Reforms for Rapid Improvement, Strong Performers and Successful Reformers in Education: Lessons from PiSA for the United States," OECD 2010, accessed January 2, 2016, http://www.oecd.org/pisa/pisaproducts/46581323.pdf, 202.
3. "Germany: Key Findings, PISA Results from PISA 2012," OECD 2012, accessed January 2, 2016, http://www.oecd.org/pisa/keyfindings/PISA-2012-results-germany.pdf, 1. This is also supported in an Atlantic article: Carly Berwick, "The Great German School Turnaround," The Atlantic Online, November 3, 2015, http://www.theatlantic.com/education/archive/2015/11/great-german-scool-turnaround/413806/.
4. To see the breakdown in government funding as it relates to education, please see: "Policy Basics: Where Do Our State Tax Dollars Go?," Center for Budget and Policy Priorities, April 14, 2015, http://www.cbpp.org/research/policy-basics-where-do-our-state-tax-dollars-go. And for a survey

showing that education is viewed as a "top priority" to most Americans, please see this Gallup poll that claims that the second highest priority to Americans after the economy is education, with 81 percent of Americans viewing education as "Extremely/Very Important." Frank Newport and Joy Wilke, "Americans Rate Economy as Top Priority for Government," Gallup Online, January 16, 2014,http://www.gallup.com/poll/166880/americans-rate-economy-top-priority-government.aspx.

5. "United States: Key Findings, PISA Results from PISA 2012," OECD 2012, accessed January 2, 2016, http://www.oecd.org/pisa/keyfindings/PISA-2012-results-US.pdf, 1.

16

Let Us Model Our Learning Culture Movement on Other Successful Social Change Movements

The Civil Rights Movement

Why We Can't Wait is Martin Luther King's book in which he shares the importance of his nonviolence philosophy in fighting against segregation, and he specifically chronicles the pivotal Birmingham freedom campaign of 1963. When reading his book along with Taylor Branch's Pulitzer Prize winning book, *Parting The Waters: America in the King Years, 1954–1963,* one can "feel" the depths of the challenge King and his lieutenants faced in trying to get America to change. The Birmingham campaign was especially critical. During the spring of 1963, the Civil Rights Movement was at an impasse. The Kennedy administration's civil rights bill was losing steam and Dr. King was searching for a way to bring momentum to the movement. When he arrived in Birmingham, he and his aides were surprised to find little community interest in participating in a march. Birmingham Public Safety Commissioner Bull Connor had an iron grip on the city, leaving supporters afraid to speak out. Wary of how things would turn out, before the march began, King was prepared for it to fail.[1]

Then, something amazing happened.

Young black Birmingham children responded and skipped school to join Dr. King in his march for freedom. When police heard of the children's plans to attend, they nailed some of the doors and windows of schools shut to keep them from attending the march. The children, however, burst through the barriers to attend.

Bull Conner arrested countless children that day, crowding them into cells, as many as seventy-five children in cells made for eight people. But that did not stop them. On the second day, a thousand more children marched. Conner brought out the fire hoses and dogs and Americans saw brutal discrimination, and the rest is history. The civil rights bill passed the next year. Taylor Branch calls the Birmingham campaign *The Children's Miracle,* because, indeed, that is what it was.[2]

The Environmental Movement

A well-researched Sonoma State University paper revealed the following:

> Environmentalism is the most popular social movement in the United States today. Five million American households contribute to national environmental organizations, which together receive over $350 million in contributions from all sources. On the local level some six thousand environmental groups are active. Seventy-five percent of Americans in 1989 identified themselves as environmentalists—all the more remarkable given that twenty-five years before there were no "environmentalists" and ecology was an obscure branch of biological science. In 1965 there were no more than a half-dozen national conservation organizations with citizen members and some degree of influence, and most were on a shaky financial footing. Although conservationists were beginning to win important victories preserving wilderness and protecting air and water from pollution, no one anticipated the explosion of activism that was about to take place.[3]

How did that happen? How did the environmental movement grow to its current status as a social movement leader? Some would say that legislative accomplishments such as the Clean Air Act, the Endangered Species Act, and a host of other laws helped the country pay more attention to issues pertaining to the environment. Others suggest that Rachel Carson's *Silent Spring* was the catalyst that was needed.[4] Still others point to the creation of Earth Day in 1970 as the moment when the world community came together and began to pay attention to the well-being of our planet.[5]

From my viewpoint, all of those things contributed to us being more environmentally conscious. But, standing alone, those things did not propel us to becoming an environmentally concerned community. Rather, the environment became our most popular social movement when it was fashionably ingrained into our popular culture. By using part marketing, part branding, part messaging, and part "cool factor" tactics, environmentalists changed the nature of the discussion from "look what they are doing to our planet" to "this is what I can do to make a change." In other words, as soon as average, everyday citizens believed that they had the power to make a difference, they began to act differently in their own lives and our culture began to change.

For instance, when I was young, my friends did not give a second thought to littering. It was commonplace to see Coke cans, candy wrappers, or McDonald's bags hurled into the street. Today, not only do fewer people litter, but, more significantly, regular citizens will not hesitate to intervene when they see someone litter. I have seen people yell, honk their horns, and threaten to call the police when they witness someone littering.

This approach that ties the individual's actions to the environment applies to our children as well. After years of seeing their favorite stars talk about the environment on the Disney Channel, Nickelodeon, and popular children's magazines, most children growing up today actually *think* about the impact of their actions on the environment. From minimizing running water from the faucet to recycling paper products to knowing what a "green" community looks like, our children have become the environmental movement's secret weapon. By the late 1980s and early 1990s, environmental responsibility became a buzzword that moved people to consider the environmental impacts of everything from how we do business and how we create government to how we make choices in our daily lives. And more recently, with further advocates speaking up and bringing the environment to the main stage, such as Bill McKibben and Al Gore, the movement has become more than just that and is a big part of the national dialogue and culture.[6]

Gay Rights Movement

Modern human rights movements are not only using popular culture to leverage social change, but also using traditional entertainment formats and the power of their narrative attributes to engage mass audiences to question their existing realities and mobilize to make that social change happen. "Pop culture with a purpose." Edutainment strategies have the power to affect the collective consciousness of societies and bring about long-term social change.

Possibly the best example of using edutainment and employing pop culture with a purpose strategy was the landmark television series "Will & Grace." The Gay Rights Movement gained significant cultural influence thanks to these mainstream shows launched in the late 1990s that purposely showed members of the LGBT community engaged in traditional social and family situations, making them relatable across liberal and conservative households.

The subtle, simple messaging was brilliant: Rather than focus on more controversial issues that challenge taken-for-granted norms in American society, the Gay Rights movement, like the Civil Rights and Women's Rights Movements in the past, asked to be included in already accepted structures and traditional social norms, that is, join the military or get married and start a family. That focus on inclusion and equality appealed to both conservatives and liberals and contained an inherent fairness message that made sense. "Will & Grace" was seen as a critical part of this effort.[7]

Public Health Movement

Another earlier and more outright example of the edutainment approach was South Africa's Soul City television series that launched in 1994. The Soul City television drama series is part of a multimedia health promotion and social change project by the Soul City Institute for Health and Development Communication (SC IHDC). Set in the fictional Soul City Township, South Africa, the Soul City series mirrors the social and development challenges faced by poor communities everywhere. It weaves health and social issues into real-life stories for the millions of people who have grown to trust the powerful messages of this very popular program. Through drama, the series changes social norms, attitudes, and practice, and gives power to individuals and communities to make informed healthy choices.[8]

Technology's Role in Enacting Social Change

Before we can change our culture, however, we need to understand what culture means, how it emerges, how it develops, and how it can be changed. Our culture represents who we are and is a reflection of societal beliefs, customs, mores, and our way of life. Culture is fluid;

it is always changing. Naturally, cultural changes can be driven by social movements. Civil rights, women's rights, gay rights all have led to enormous changes in the way we view each of these issues, which is reflected in our current culture.

Throughout all of these cultural shifts, most Americans *assumed* that our education system was as reliable as our democracy itself. Our approach to education has been viewed as part of the foundational fabric of our society. As a result, until recently when the reality of our educational shortfalls got greater attention, our educational system has been somewhat immune to changes in our culture. But two things are changing that historical perspective: technology and the media.

Technological innovations, social media, and societal globalization can enhance or accelerate changes in our culture. Savvy branding and marketing experts know this. So they constantly use those tools to imbed an idea, hawk a product, or change a point of view. And it all can happen quickly. There are many ways to change culture while utilizing the technologies of today, a few of which I will discuss below.

The Learning Culture Movement

From environmentalism to gay and civil rights, all of these movements can be tied to all of the factors I mentioned earlier, but perhaps what is most striking is the idea that these movements evolved not out of particular actions or events, but out of a larger cultural change. The 1960s and 1970s were a time of great social change, and much of this can be tied back to the idea that the individual matters, namely, the belief that an individual voice rising up and taking a stand against a larger bureaucratic power can actually make a difference. It was with the counterculture movement of these decades that individuals realized their power and recognized that they could make a difference.[9] Sounds familiar? This is not at all unlike what I have been advocating about education: develop a culture of learning that not only focuses on and champions the individual, but is borne out of actions taken by individuals as well. All it takes is one group of parents to recognize their power to change their children's education for a national movement to arise. And the actions and ideas of individuals really take flight when pop culture and the media are behind them. So, how do we marry today's popular cultural influences with individuals' desires to build a new learning culture? The influence of the media plays a huge role in culture change, and it is time for us to strategically examine more ways in which the media can be utilized to spread the right messages and feature the right images around learning.

It may be hard at first for us to imagine a common theme between academic achievement and *Duck Dynasty*, *The Kardashians*, or the various Housewives reality shows. But what about a reality show such as *Garage High*? This program spotlights children who are going through trade-based charter and alternative schools and learning auto-mechanics. Each season follows one group of mechanics from one school, so the viewer grows attached to these teens. The team is partnered with a famous mechanic and they work side by side fixing cars for the community. The cars they produce are given away to low-income families or auctioned, with the proceeds going to educate disadvantaged students. Think of the potential sponsors: NASCAR, AutoZone, Pennzoil? Or imagine a program modeled after the popular home improvement shows in which the host and his team pick a couple of the notoriously failing schools in small town America, organize a first-rate team of great educators, and lead the viewers to the complete revamping of the school?

Better still, how about a show modeled after *American Idol*, but focusing on education instead—we could call it *America's Best School*. I have been working with a team of talented individuals to develop a television program that will be built around student video nominations from around the country in an effort to "find America's best school." Students will be excited to nominate their schools to be on television and, similar to *American Idol*, each week audiences will be introduced to a nominated school and its approach. Along with a couple of well-known panelists, they will get to decide which schools will move on to star in upcoming episodes. As the season progresses and the number of schools dwindles, the celebrity judges will visit the schools, interviewing students and teachers on why their school deserves to win the grand prize. With these kinds of programs, all of a sudden, education and learning becomes cool.

The point is that we need to engage real people with things that they can relate to in order to bring education and learning into their day-to-day lives. That cannot be accomplished by way of politics or policy debates. We must make education cool, fun, and popular. And, similar to the approaches utilized by social movements from our recent past, we must be intentional, strategic, and forward thinking in how we use popular culture to build our learning culture.

As we think about how to reshape American education into a learning culture, many of those same strategies used to influence popular culture are infinitely transferable. It begins with smartly and strategically leveraging traditional and new media, such as social media and emerging technologies, to reach people where they are, to tap into their interests. Here, however, we take that approach to excite the possibilities of learning, make it fun, cool, and meaningful in ways that they never imagined. In the past, most people thought of education connected to an education system. Through popular culture, we can demonstrate to all Americans that the power of learning is an individual undertaking that doesn't have to be dictated by a system or group-think. Instead, through real-life popular examples, the learner receives constant positive reinforcement just by working hard at his or her pace and feels empowered about his or her progress each step of the way. Our learning culture of tomorrow should always place a premium on individual learning accomplishments as a natural way to motivate others to do the same.

Notes

1. Taylor Branch, *Parting the Waters: America in the King Years 1954–63* (New York: Simon & Schuster, 1988), 756.
2. Taylor Branch, *Parting the Waters*, 757–58.
3. David Walls, "Environmental Movement," Sonoma State University, accessed January 2, 2016, http://www.sonoma.edu/users/w/wallsd/environmental-movement.shtml.
4. Eliza Griswold, "How 'Silent Spring' Ignited the Environmental Movement," *The New York Times* Online, September 21, 2012, http://www.nytimes.com/2012/09/23/magazine/how-silent-spring-ignited-the-environmental-movement.html.
5. "Earth Day: History of a Movement," Earth Day Network, accessed January 2, 2016, http://www.earthday.org/earth-day-history-movement.
6. "Global Consumers Vote Al Gore, Oprah Winfrey and Kofi Annan Most Influential to Champion Global Warming Cause: A Nielsen Survey," Market Research World, July 7, 2007, http://www.marketresearchworld.net/content/view/1394/77/.
7. Abby Rogers, "'Will & Grace' Creator Explains How He Created a Successful Gay TV Show Using Ellen's Mistakes,"*Business Insider*, February 5, 2013,

http://www.businessinsider.com/max-mutchnick-explains-will-and-grace-2013-2.

8. H. Perlman, S. Usdin, and J. Button, "Using Popular Culture for Social Change: Soul City Videos and a Mobile Clip for Adolescents in South Africa," *Reproductive Health Matters* 21, no. 41 (May 2013): 31–34. doi: 10.1016/S0968-8080(13)41707-X, http://www.ncbi.nlm.nih.gov/pubmed/23684184. For more information on the success of the Soul City project, you can check out their site here: http://www.soulcity.org.za/projects/soul-city-series.

9. "In Praise of the Counterculture," *The New York Times* Online, December 11, 1994, http://www.nytimes.com/1994/12/11/opinion/in-praise-of-the-counterculture.html.

17

Trusted Voices Championing the Cause

In 2012, I visited the Jalen Rose Leadership Academy Charter School in the former basketball star's hometown of Detroit, Michigan. While taking a tour of the school, Jalen told me about what motivated him to start his own school. "I grew up in this community," he said. "I know these kids. I was once one of these kids. But if it weren't for basketball, I could easily be a statistic. But like me, so many of these kids can be a success. We just have to give them hope and show them the way. I am determined to use my celebrity to make a difference."

And he has. Detroit has one of the worst educational outputs for children in the nation. In the past, Detroit has had the lowest graduation rate in the country, with only 25 percent of students graduating from high school.[1] Jalen's school is educating children who otherwise would not be educated. But it hasn't been easy. Jalen went through four principals during the first four years of his school. The proof, however, was in the pudding. When his school had its first graduation in 2015, all ninety-three graduates were going to college.

Jalen is not alone. More and more celebrities are lending their name and their influence to the cause of education and learning in America. What is really exciting about this new phenomenon is that the celebs are not tied to the politics of the establishment. They just want to help children. Additionally, so many of these celebs relate directly to these children's lives. The celebrity urge to lend a hand can be an extremely beneficial tool in getting children excited about learning. Even those who have lost hope.

Mega entertainer Armando Perez (whose stage name is Pitbull) knows the streets of Miami well. He came from a broken home and did not like school. He has told me repeatedly that he could have liked school, but he felt that no one cared about him at the schools he attended. Except one of his teachers, Hope Martinez. Ms. Martinez (as Armando still refers to her) saw something in him that no one else saw. She believed in him and his talent. Without Armando's knowledge, Ms. Martinez signed him up for a highly publicized rap battle that was coming to Miami. Some of the biggest names in hip hop were going to participate, and novice rappers who signed up would have the chance to battle toe to toe with the nation's best. Armando would have never signed up on his own. As good as he was, he didn't have the confidence to do so. Reluctantly, Armando went to the event (though he almost walked out several times before they called his name to perform) and blew everyone away. The rest, as they say, is history. I have seen Armando share his story with groups of low-income and forgotten children in Miami: children like him. When he talks about Ms. Martinez and the value of an education and the value of having someone believe in you, you can hear a pin drop. Often, as he shares his story, a tear or two emerges when he talks about his former teacher and he always tells the children, "I believe in you."

Working with Academica's Fernando Zulueta, Armando started the Sports Leadership and Management (SLAM) charter school in downtown Miami. SLAM uses sports themes as an innovate learning tool throughout its curriculum. For instance, math teachers use the dimensions of football and soccer fields to help teach math. A biology class may reference a famous injured pro star as they look at the structure of the knee. Even for children who are not athletes, SLAM makes learning fun. And never discount the cool factor. In leading Academica to becoming one of the most successful charter school networks in the country, Fernando has opened well over hundred schools. He shakes his head when he says, "SLAM is the first school I opened in which the children were bringing the parents to the school, not the other way around. There were children who caught buses from the other side of town and forged their parents' signature to try to get enrolled in the school. I have never seen anything like it!"

Yes, the cool factor matters. Working with the American Federation for Children (AFC) and Jalen Rose, we organized a group of celebs who were eager to speak out in favor of educational choice. Basketball star and Olympiad Lisa Leslie got involved, as did football legend Deion Sanders. The group led our development of a public service announcement in which famous faces say it is time for educational choice. Folks like Shaquille O'Neal, Louis Gossett, Jr., Kathie Lee Gifford, Vivica Fox, Laila Ali, Olympic swimmer Janet Evans, Cosby kid Keisha Knight-Pulliam, and others. Posters were made of the stars with an attached message on it. These posters were placed in beauty shops, barber shops, grocery stores, and neighborhood businesses in selected states where AFC does its work. The response was incredible. It's one thing if I advocate for more quality options for our children; it's another if Shaquille O'Neal, Vivica Fox, or Pitbull is delivering the message. The same holds true for the growing number of stars who are getting more directly involved in education. For instance, Andre Agassi devotes most of his time to the charter school he founded in his hometown of Las Vegas; as does boxer Oscar De La Hoya, who founded a highly successful charter school in east Los Angeles. John Legend is on the boards of Teach for America, Stand for Children, and the Harlem Village Learning Academies.

We need to be more and more intentional about using these trusted voices to get America excited about learning. People listen to entertainers, athletes, and celebrities. We must also be creative. I envision using celebs to help brand education differently, by highlighting that cool factor. Positive, upbeat messaging; slick ad campaigns; friendly, competitive learning challenges—all these things push us toward the upbeat learning culture we need. We must work to channel these celebrities' desire to make a difference into positive messages extolling the virtues of creating personal and national pride around learning. Our children's education doesn't just belong to educators. We need more trusted voices and influencers who are ready, willing, and able to be advocates for education. These voices are crucial ingredients to building our new learning culture.

Note

1. "Detroit Has Worst High School Graduation Rate," NPR, June 29, 2007, http://www.npr.org/templates/story/story.php?storyId=11601692.

18

Celebrating Models and Teachers That Work

One of the most rewarding aspects of my work is that I have visited schools all across America, schools that are doing an incredible job educating our children. Usually, however, the great work that so many of these schools are doing is not as well known as it should be. Everyone knows about Columbine because of the shootings that took place at that school. CNN made sure of that. Yet few people outside of select schools' local areas have heard of the many great schools that are doing great work for children. The same holds true for the many great teachers who work their magic in their class-rooms each and every day. These schools and their teachers need to be celebrated, lifted up, exalted.

In sharing more broadly the unique and remarkable work being done by many schools and their teachers, we shine a spotlight on innovation and creativity that others normally do not see. In our new learning culture, we should remain curious about new and different approaches to teaching and learning. My curiosity has led me to innumerable schools from coast to coast. Public, private, parochial, public charter, independent, religious, specialty, magnet, I have seen them all. The good ones definitely stand out.

As we shine a light on outstanding schools and teachers, we must shed our own "school label" baggage. By school label, I am refer-ring to the type of school: private, public, public charter, religious, independent, and the like. We are so used to instinctively reacting or forming opinions based on the label attached to a school, we block ourselves from the important question: Does this school or learning environment work for children? Here is a case in point.

Several years ago, BAEO president Ken Campbell and I had dinner in Mobile, Alabama, with about twelve members of the

Alabama Legislative Black Caucus. We were meeting with them to talk about charter schools. Alabama is one of eight states that do not have a charter school law. During dinner, we had a very lively, even jovial, discussion about schools, children, and teachers. Nearly each one of the legislators had a host of complaints about the local school districts in the areas they represented. One legislator, in particular, talked about the challenges he had with his grandson's school. He bemoaned the fact that there was no accountability at the school; that the bad teachers keep teaching with no intervention or professional development; that the principal has no autonomy— the district would not let her run her school; that parents feel so unwelcome at the school—they are just plain helpless. He even said that if it were not for his position and influence, his grandson would be lost. But even with that influence, he stated, it is a day-to-day struggle.

Ken and I then started to talk about our own experiences. Ken is a fabulous education expert. He worked with me in DC when we started charter schools while he was working with the DC Board of Trade. He helped start our incubator program which helped prepare new charter schools for their opening day. Ken also worked at building schools in Qatar before running the charter school office in Louisiana. A cofounder of BAEO, he has been its president for several years. Since I helped guide the push for the scholarship program in Louisiana, Ken and I complimented each other well. We had been integrally involved in the two most educational choice-friendly jurisdictions in the country. There wasn't a question we could not answer.

After the two of us parried off question after question, it was clear that several members were warming to our arguments. At that point, the legislator who had been complaining about his grandson's school blurted out: "All that sounds good, but I will not support charter schools in Alabama. I do not believe in charter schools!"

By then, I had learned my lesson from my earlier experience with the South Carolina Black Caucus. I took a different approach.

I said, "Mr. Representative, I understand your concerns. Let's not talk about charter schools. Let's assume that I agree with you. Charter schools do not need to be in the state of Alabama. Instead, let's talk about your grandson's school." Looking around the room,

I continued, "let's talk about all of your children's schools. Why don't you, Mr. Representative, draft a bill that will help all of these children. Let's call it the Representative ___ (his name) bill for better schools. In the bill, why don't you change the current law so that classroom teachers are more accountable. Include some provisions that give principals more authority to move out the bad teachers. Speaking of principals, you should include in your bill a mechanism for giving principals more freedoms from the local school district central office. The bill should give them more autonomy over their building and the ability to access supplies easier. Also, try to include a better avenue for parents to sign up for schools and gain access to their children's teachers and the school leaders. Why don't you put together that bill with your name on it and introduce it. Don't include the words 'charter school' anywhere in the bill. It's your bill. Now, in DC and Louisiana, we call that type of legislation charter school legislation, but, here in Alabama, let's just call it your bill."

Some of the other members smiled, as did Ken. The legislator, to whom I was speaking, said, "I like the sound of that bill, but I still don't like charter schools."

Fortunately, in 2013, Alabama passed a statewide private school scholarship bill for low-income children and in the next year finally passed the long fought-over charter school legislation.

Like it or not, labels matter. As we transition to a national community of learners—rather than individuals feeding into separate and distinct educational systems—our emphasis must be on the richness of the learning environment as opposed to the source of the provider.

In 2013, I was asked by the Education Writers of America to attend their annual conference which was scheduled to take place at Stanford University. They had also invited Randi Weingarten, the president of the *American Federation for Teachers* (AFT), to attend as well. The group's organizers wanted Randi and me to participate in a debate over whether or not educational choice is a good thing. Later described as a heavyweight fight by a reporter who covered the debate, Randi and I went toe to toe on a host of issues. Most notably, she maintained that charters, vouchers, and school choice alternatives were a distraction; that we should invest in what we know works. Conversely, I countered that we know what doesn't work and how long do parents have to wait for us to study the study, plan the plan, and debate the debate over what works while their children are trapped in schools that do not work for them? We went back and forth like that for over an hour.

The essence of Randi's "charters and choice are a distraction" argument is the common refrain I hear all the time from folks immersed within the status quo: we should spend our time and energy helping all the children as opposed to finding options that work for just a few. That line of thinking, along with the other common argument that decries choice because "all the children do not benefit," has led to intense and bitter resistance to system change. It also fuels the lethargy of waiting for schools to improve. The system will get there. Just trust us and wait. But still, all the thinking revolves around the system.

I had a similar discussion with Education Secretary Arne Duncan while we both happened to be on the same flight from DC to St. Louis. As soon as he saw me, he began to chat me up about my advocacy for the DCOSP. His approach was less hostile than Eric Holder's, and we ended up having a very fruitful conversation while standing in the back of the plane. One dicey moment came as he became exasperated with my failure to understand the big picture involving reforming our education system. He said, "Kevin, the DCOSP provides scholarships for only 2,000 students. I have the responsibility to make sure we are educating the 56 million American children who are in school. We have to focus on the things that work."

In response, I said, "I get that, Mr. Secretary. I really do. But, I look at it differently. With each of those 56 million children, there is an individual story. A story that can easily get lost when looking at them as numbers on a page. We need to focus on the educational needs of each and every child. If we can't provide a high quality education to those 2,000 DCOSP children, or even worse, we take a good education away from them, we don't have the standing or right to educate 56 million other children."

At that point, the two secret service agents came to the back of the plane to see if the secretary was "alright." Arne smiled and we continued to chat amiably, agreeing to agree in most areas, while agreeing to disagree in others.

I do believe that Arne Duncan wants to do the right thing for children and that he is a reformer. But, interestingly, the feeling of the need to focus only on what works, with the idea to scale it up in a way to change our education system, is prevalent among many education reformers and is in many ways similar to what Randi Weingarten argues. Some years ago, several major education reform philanthropists got together to discuss charter school networks that work and education reform proposals that make sense. They, like others in the education reform world, were focused on "scaling up" the things that have been proven to be successful. In other words, if we all can focus on a handful of successful approaches and support them and fund them more aggressively, we can then bring changes in education to scale. As a result, many who have been fighting for education reform for years are now totally focused on education management organizations (EMOs) and charter school management organizations (CMOs) that can quickly churn out large numbers of schools that contain their unique and proven approach. I support those efforts—with one cautionary thought. In our zeal to scale up what works, we must be very careful not to become overly excited with one approach or a handful of approaches. Adopting that focus is not different from Randi's approach: both are centered on promoting a "system" that works. But neither promotes an organic, grassroots, community-based culture of learning that is ongoing and flexible to the unique needs of a district or region.

Of course there are several EMOs and CMOs that are able to do both: grow a cluster of schools that work for children and create a culture of learning that is ongoing. Those organizations, however, have found a way to have enough flexibility in their approach so that it is adaptable, depending on the characteristics, needs, and nuances associated with the location of the school. One such organization is the Miami-based Academica, one of the most successful and enterprising charter school operators and education service providers in the country. Founded in 1999 by attorney and businessman Fernando Zulueta, Academica now has over hundred schools in its network of schools. While the bulk of Academica's schools are in south Florida, they also have schools in California, Texas, Nevada, Georgia, Utah, and the District of Columbia. Academica also boasts of a unique international dual diploma program in which students from foreign countries can obtain a US high-school diploma through Academica's Somerset Virtual Academy International Dual Diploma Program. I spoke with fourteen-year-old Maria from San Sebastián, Spain, who gushed excitedly about how her US degree was going to help her into a better college—all without setting foot in the United States.

But the heart of Academica's success lies in its K-12 offerings for US students. The academic success of most of Academica's south Florida-managed schools is nothing short of remarkable. Academica's Florida schools are regularly among the best performing high schools in the state. And the vast majority of the students in Academica's network are minority children who qualify for free or reduced lunch. In 2014, nine Academica-serviced schools were on the US News and World Reports Best High Schools List. Quite simply, Academica is by far one of the best networks of schools consistently getting strong academic results from the most challenged group of students.

According to Fernando Zulueta, Academica's success flows from its core belief that each individual school must create its own learning culture that's compatible with and complimentary to the community it serves. As such, Fernando strongly adheres to the stated Academica operating principle "that each charter school is a unique educational environment governed by an independent Board of Directors that best knows the right path for its school, and Academica's mission is to facilitate that Governing Board's vision." In practice, each Academica-managed school gives almost complete control of the school to the principal and the local board. They are given goals, timetables, and bench marks for student achievement and all the resources they need. Then, they are measured by their results, which since 1999 have been stellar. Fernando completely shuns the tactic used by some education management service providers in which they dictate the same approach to each of the schools within their portfolio. How is that approach different from the cookie cutter one-size-fits-all model we have been trying to change in many traditional public schools? Fernando and his Academica team understand that in order to truly build a national learning culture to scale, it must be locally nurtured and grown from the bottom up, community by community. As a result, Academica may have the most empowered, autonomous, and successful group of principals in the country: principals who have successfully created a culture of learning.

*   *   *

In lifting up models that work, we must also hold our effective teachers in higher esteem. Yes, the teaching profession is viewed positively by nearly everyone, but many teachers are still not accorded the respect that they deserve. Some would suggest that the challenges in many of our schools have damaged the reputation of the teaching profession. I believe that what has damaged teachers the most are the bad teachers. Even one bad teacher, like one bad apple, can spoil the reputation of the whole bunch. Teachers have also been hurt by the lack of consistency found in most school districts pertaining to professional development. It is easy to see why some teachers get burned out when many get little, if any, direct substantive feedback, professional development is minimal, and room for advancement within the profession has limits.

When I debated Randi Weingarten at the education writers conference, she had to concede one major point when I began to talk about *A Nation at Risk* and its recommendations. After pointing out that virtually none of the commission's thirty-eight recommendations have been adopted, I challenged Randi about the handful of recommendations made regarding teachers and teaching. "One of the recommendations said that we should move to professionalize our teaching corp," I said. "Why haven't you done that Randi?" "That's a good point, Kevin," she said in response. "We do need to professionalize our teachers."

Sadly, it still has not been done. Unfortunate. For us to become a community of learners, the great schools and teachers have to be treasured and showcased as examples to admire and to follow. One of the most common traits shared by great teachers is that they do their work anonymously. That must change.

Clearly, the commission of *A Nation at Risk* put considerable time and attention on the issue of teaching and America's teaching corp when they deliberated their recommendations over thirty years ago. The commission recommended that we professionalize America's teachers in order to ensure that teachers continue to be held at the highest standards possible and that the education world starts to treat them with more professional respect. The recommendations included the following:

- Persons preparing to teach should be required to meet high educational standards, to demonstrate an aptitude for teaching, and to demonstrate competence in an academic discipline. Colleges and universities offering teacher preparation programs should be judged by how well their graduates meet these criteria.
- Salaries for the teaching profession should be increased and should be professionally competitive, market-sensitive, and performance-based. Salary, promotion, tenure, and retention decisions should be tied to an effective evaluation system that includes peer review so that superior teachers can be rewarded, average ones encouraged, and poor ones either improved or terminated.
- School boards should adopt an 11-month contract for teachers. This would ensure time for curriculum and professional development, programs for students with special needs, and a more adequate level of teacher compensation.
- School boards, administrators, and teachers should cooperate to develop career ladders for teachers that distinguish among the beginning instructor, the experienced teacher, and the master teacher.
- Substantial nonschool personnel resources should be employed to help solve the immediate problem of the shortage of mathematics and science teachers. Qualified individuals, including recent graduates with mathematics and science degrees, graduate students, and industrial and retired scientists, could, with appropriate preparation, immediately begin teaching in these fields. A number of our leading science centers have the capacity to begin educating and retraining teachers immediately. Other areas of critical teacher need, such as English, must also be addressed.
- Incentives, such as grants and loans, should be made available to attract outstanding students to the teaching profession, particularly in those areas of critical shortage.
- Master teachers should be involved in designing teacher preparation programs and in supervising teachers during their probationary years.[1]

Much has been written, both pro and con, about the idea of professionalizing teachers. Randi Weingarten's AFT tends to support the idea, while other organizations have tended to oppose it.[2] Of course, the elephant in the room is tenure, the longstanding device used to protect teachers from overzealous administrators on one hand, but unwittingly allows too many bad or marginal teachers to stay on the job and in the classroom solely based on seniority.

I agree that we should move in the direction of professionalizing teachers, but, like many things in the education policy world, the ongoing debate leads to more systems-speak and inertia.

Similar to our need to focus on individual learners as opposed to systems, we must also empower individual teachers who embrace innovation and creativity. To that end, more and more teachers are utilizing technology and experiential learning techniques to reach children they might not otherwise reach.

The traditional stand, deliver, and lecture format of teaching to students who are supposed to take notes, memorize, and regurgitate back what they have been told just doesn't work today. Plus, it is no fun. The future of learning is found in these experiential practices and problem solving. Well-known Richmond, Virginia, teacher John Hunter exploded traditional teaching methods when he taught his "World Peace Games" to his students. For over thirty years, his students have fearlessly tackled global problems and found surprising solutions through playing his World Peace Game. These children from high school down to fourth grade, in schools both well funded and under resourced, take on the role of politicians, tribal leaders, diplomats, bankers, and military commanders. Through battles and negotiations, standoffs and summits, they strive to resolve dozens of complex, seemingly intractable real-world challenges from nuclear proliferation to tribal warfare, financial collapse to climate change. The results are always astounding and, as John Hunter maintains, every country has more than it had before the game started and that the world is a better place. Or in other words, the children end up solving the problems that the adults have yet to solve.[3]

Indeed, now when I visit schools and chat with students, I channel John Hunter's amazing style and take Googler Jaime Casap's suggestion by never asking children, "What do you want to be when you grow up?" Rather, as I visit schools all over America, I always ask children, "What problems do you want to solve?" In starting conversations with children with that question, I always get engaged and excited discussions going. Taking that approach also leads to some pretty incredible problem-solving ideas. For example, I asked the question, "What problem do you want to solve?" to a group of sixth graders at a Catholic elementary school near downtown Charleston, South Carolina. One eleven-year-old girl raised her hand and began to talk about the way the homeless were treated by officials supposedly providing them with food and other services. She was particularly incensed by how the police and the folks running the shelter near her school would let the food line go into the street, which led to many homeless citizens vulnerable to possibly being hit by rush hour traffic. She suggested that they guide the line in another direction, away from the street, and that they use volunteers from the high school located in the same block to help serve the food and obtain the needed intake information. Apparently, she had already been getting names of potential volunteers from her sister, a student at the high school. And that was just the beginning of her comments regarding her ideas on the subject. After the class ended, the teacher pulled me aside and said that she was flabbergasted by the level of thought that the girl had given to the issue. The teacher further said that she was calling city officials to have them sit down with the girl to hear her ideas. I was glad that I asked the original question.

In appealing to our collective higher selves, the real solution centers on finding ways to exalt good teachers, irrespective of the teaching style or approach they choose to employ, and reward them more broadly, as Brian Crosby suggested in his book, *The $100,000 Teacher: A Solution to America's Declining Public School System*, by creatively, yet strategically elevating their statute in society.[4] For instance, what if each Ivy League school, or the most influential colleges in a given state (like the university president I spoke with on the plane), agreed to endow a rotating visiting professor chair for the area's K-12 teacher of the year? Or those designated as master teachers are automatically assigned a group of peers they can coach, similar to Carol Keenan's approach at Salemwood, as you will see in the next chapter. Or airlines and other businesses agree to give master teachers a 10 percent discount on all flights or travel. These and other ideas, of course, would come with additional compensation. As we build our new culture of learning, the possibilities for uplifting teachers' societal status are endless. Within the profession, young, good teachers would have something to aspire to beyond just years in the same classroom with little or no recognition. Outside of the profession, we must begin to more prominently hold up these teachers as symbols of excellence—all with a view toward creating a profession that is viewed as desirable and meaningful. The bottom line is that in our new learning-rich environment, being a great teacher should mean a whole lot more than it does now, both among peers and in society as a whole. But let's also give deference to Carol Keenan's sage words of advice. When school leaders take care of the simple things for their teachers and engage their day-to-day needs in a collaborative way, teachers are empowered and children benefit. By supporting teachers in and out of the classroom, we increase their productivity and help elevate the profession.

Our need to celebrate learning, give greater community attention to models and teachers that work, and create a national obsession around learning is a far cry from the education discussions of today. Nearly everything we talk about in education is discussed in a negative context. Failing schools, achievement gaps, and not measuring up academically as a nation. And yes, I can point out those deficits as well as anyone. But at some point our education discussions must *evolve*. We cannot remain mired in the muck. Even our debates about standards have devolved into political side-choosing and concerns over states' rights. When our leaders exacerbate these tensions, our children suffer.

During the height of the debate over the common core standards, I wrote a blog post that appeared in *Education Week*, entitled *This Toxic Standards Fight Isn't Helping Students*. In the blog I wrote the following:

> I respect education policy debate and discussion, but the division and bickering around the standards has me "sick and tired." Not only are we embroiled in a growing verbal death match, but partisan politics has once again taken precedence over doing what's right for kids. I see this firsthand as I travel from state to state, discussing education reform and the importance of educational choice with legislators and local community leaders. Increasingly, where one stands on the common-core debate is a new political litmus test akin to one's political party bona fides.[5]

Time after time, we default back to taking sides at our children's expense. How about joining hands for their benefit? While we can agree to disagree on many education policy issues, shouldn't we also be able to agree to lift up the things that work: those schools and teachers that grow learning? Employing this approach is a critical component of building a learning culture in America.

Notes

1. "A Nation at Risk: Recommendations," US Department of Education, April 1983, https://www2.ed.gov/pubs/NatAtRisk/recomm.html.
2. "History," American Federation of Teachers, accessed January 2, 2016, http://www.aft.org/about/history.
3. To learn more about John Hunter's teaching style and the success of his "World Peace Games," you can watch this TED Talk: John Hunter, "Teaching with the World Peace Game," TED Talks TED2011, March 2011, accessed January 4, 2016, https://www.ted.com/talks/john_hunter_on_the_world_peace_game?language=en or check out the World Peace Games website: http://www.worldpeacegame.org.
4. Brian Crosby, *The $100,000 Teacher: A Teacher's Solution to America's Declining Public School System* (Sterling: Capital Books, 2002), 6.
5. Kevin P. Chavous, "This Toxic Standards Fight Isn't Helping Students," *Education Week*, April 11, 2014, http://www.edweek.org/ew/articles/2014/04/11/28chavous.h33.html.

Part 3

Some Success Stories

19

Three Schools and One School District with Great Teachers and a Learning Culture

All across America there are countless schools—public, public charter, and private—that have established learning cultures for the students they serve and the communities in which they operate. Not only should we celebrate these schools, but we must learn from them. These schools are key to building a new national learning culture, especially because these schools built their respective learning cultures from the bottom up.

Salemwood School

The Salemwood School is a K-8 school located in Malden, Massachusetts, just outside of Boston. Salemwood is a traditional public school within the Malden School District. Of the 1,225 children attending the school, 83 percent are on free or reduced lunch, and the school boasts of a highly diverse population of students: 27 percent white, 26 percent African American, 28 percent Hispanic, 19 percent other.[1]

When I visited the school, I had already heard about the solid academic proficiency at Salemwood, something that is often rare for a traditional school with the same demographics. I also knew that part of the school's success was attributable to their relationship with the Bay State reading program founded by Ed Moscovitch. That highly successful program works with teachers to make sure that they consistently offer more support and time on task for students' reading. Each day, students spend 120 minutes on reading and 90 minutes on math. The teachers work with Bay State to develop ways to keep the extra time meaningful and fun for the students.[2]

But after my visit to the school where I spent several hours with a host of teachers and students, I realized that the true essence of Salemwood's success was not just in the reading program they use. Salemwood is a success because they have created a culture of learning that permeates everything they do—and it includes everyone involved with the school, be they students, parents, teachers, or staff. Much of Salemwood's success is clearly attributable to the school's principal, Carol Keenan. She is the school's rock, proving how important it is to have a strong school leader. Principal Keenan also represents the embodiment of being able to bring everyone together in a cohesive way for the betterment of children, a sentiment reflected in the school's mission found right on the school website:

> It is our vision to foster a true elementary and middle school experience for all students to prepare them to be academically and socially successful as they matriculate from kindergarten through high school.[3]

Carol is a lifelong educator and has worked in the Malden school district for nearly thirty years. Although Carol was very familiar with how school districts work with their assorted roles, responsibilities, state practices and bureaucratic practices, she was determined to create something "special" when she took over as principal at Salemwood, something that would rise above the challenges found in many school districts. Hearing her speak about her approach and vision was refreshing and enlightening. And after spending several hours with ten to twelve teachers, I was ready to genuflect to Carol Keenan. During my session with the various teachers, neither Carol nor her senior staff were present. The teachers all agreed that the school's success began with Carol. Each pointed out how the tone for the entire school was set by their principal. When Carol first became principal, the Bay State team was already in place, but it had not reached it's full potential. So Carol introduced, implemented and fostered the importance of teaming, which made Bay State much stronger. She told them that she was determined to build a new culture, one that put the learning of the children first. In the process, she emphasized to her team that this presented an opportunity for each of them to learn as well. And that the overriding goal was for everyone in the school to be better at what they do. She implemented the importance of teaming and utilizing peer coaches for her teachers; and also created new team leaders roles as well as unofficial mentors for the coaches. Managing those relationships fell under the responsibility of Literacy Coach Heather Provenzano.

In order to get some of the more senior, hesitant teachers to buy into her approach for teaching and learning, Carol met with them individually and probed about the things they each needed in order to do their jobs better. According to the teachers, Carol listens and implements what needs to be done to make the school successful; both academically and socially.

As one veteran teacher told me, "Right away, Carol immediately addressed our wants and our needs. And that has never changed. You could call her at ten o'clock at night with some issue and she will always respond the same way: yes, I can do that; no, I can't do that; or let me see what I can do. When she says she will get back with you, it is usually the next day and if she can't do it, she has thought through some alternative that makes sense. Carol works extremely collaboratively with Central Office. She is able to implement what they expect of us but in a way that makes sense for our school which again only increases student achievement. She is able to provide an environment that allows us to stay current with our craft so we can truly focus on students' learning."

And the teachers do help each other, proving Carol's teaming approach is the key. The various teams of teachers meet at least twice weekly. During those meetings, teachers discuss substantive matters ranging from how to help a struggling student to helping a peer team member with personal coaching. If any issue emerges, Carol's immediate first response is, "Have you discussed this with your team?" Generally, most issues can be addressed during the team meetings. Every single teacher has bought into the school's learning culture, even with the union work rules that give deference to seniority and make it virtually impossible to fire a bad teacher or get them out of your school. Carol has used peer pressure and the positive, "children first" work environment as a way to overcome the seniority challenges.

"When a bad teacher comes here," one teacher said, "they learn right away that they either have to step up or leave. Carol and the team leaders interview new teachers for two hours and go through various scenarios with the new teacher. They understand from the beginning that the peer teams monitor each other's classes and all teachers work long hours. Before long, those who are just going through the motions begin to feel ostracized. Sometimes, those that can change begin to step up their game. They get with the program."

For her part, Carol sees her role as the ultimate facilitator. "I have to be the liaison between the school district and my school," she says. "Central office means well, but we operate differently. We cannot afford to lose the momentum we have gained with these students."

What is most impressive about Salemwood is how infectious learning is for everyone in the building. I spoke to a janitor who said he was going back to school to take some night classes. It is impossible to spend anytime at Salemwood and not feel the urge to do something to improve yourself. The environment is completely motivating. And the attendance for both staff and students is over 95 percent. Everyone associated with the school wants to be at the school.

As to the learning culture that she and her team have established at Salemwood, Carol minimizes her role, but her influence is clear.

> When I became principal, my goal was to make things flow smoothly. The schools that work do the simple things right. So, I was committed to being as organized as possible, to take all the little things off the table so the teachers could do their jobs. I created a consistent schedule—and stuck with it; I had all the supplies in place for each teacher from day one; I stopped all loudspeaker announcements during the school day; I have answers to all of their questions—the simple things matter. I also encourage the peer groups to brainstorm ideas and to be creative. But I also remind them that every thing we do must advance student achievement. So when they come to me with a new idea or approach, they know to be prepared to make the link between the proposal and student learning. Our children's learning drives everything that we do.

As a result of Carol Keenan's approach, Salemwood has experienced an almost unheard of academic turnaround for its students. When Carol took over as principal in 2008, Salemwood was a level three school that was heading toward level four status. Massachusetts ranks schools from level one to level five, with five being the worse. The ranking is largely based on the Massachusetts Comprehensive Assessment System (MCAS) test. In just three years, Carol and her team moved Salemwood from level three to level one.[4]

The Salemwood School in Malden, Massachusetts, is a traditional public school that has created a culture of learning.

Houston Heights Learning Academy

At the Houston Heights Learning Academy Charter School (HHLA), their mission says it all:

> All children can learn and deserve the best education, one that challenges and stimulates them to discover their own unique talents, abilities, and self-worth.[5]

At HHLA, it does not take long to see that the folks who run the school live out what they say. An undeniably successful school by any measure, HHLA believes in educating the whole child and they put a strong emphasis on each child's self-worth, irrespective of the child's background. Although HHLA is a small school with only about 150 students, it provides us with a model worthy of imitation. Located in the Houston Heights community, its student body demographics is 52 percent Hispanic, 42 percent African American, 3 percent Asian, 1 percent white, and 2 percent two or more races; 98 percent of the students qualify for free or reduced lunch.[6] The school prides itself on its nurturing, friendly environment, an attitude that was more than evident when I visited the school in 2013 with former Education Secretary Rod Paige. The school has just been recognized for its academic excellence by being designated as a Title I Distinguished School for 2012. The school has always had a strong academic bent and in 2011 they accomplished something that few schools do: their students achieved a 100 percent pass rate for the Texas Assessment of Knowledge and Skills (TAKS)—the mandatory standardized test offered in Texas—in all subjects tested.[7]

In talking with the school's principal, longtime educator and former Houston public schools Principal Yvette East, it is clear that while she makes sure that her students are prepared for their tests, she is more concerned with building a learning culture among her students. Check out HHLA's stated education beliefs:

> At The Houston Heights Learning Academy we:
>
> 1) Believe that a culture of achievement promotes high student achievement.
> 2) Believe that students who are empowered with prior knowledge of assessment goals will be better prepared to take an active role in their own achievement.
> 3) Believe that high expectations promote excellence.
> 4) Believe that learning is optimized when parents and professionals work in partnership.
> 5) Believe that children have individual learning styles and intelligences that must be addressed in order for everyone to achieve.
> 6) Believe that staff members must be aware of state curriculum standards and benchmarks to maximize a student's achievement of goals.
> 7) Believe that the use of best practices reflecting current educational research increases our standard of quality.
> 8) Believe that staff members are models for our students.
> 9) Believe that staff and students are entitled to learn and work in a clean and safe environment.
> 10) Believe that a cooperative learning environment educates, empowers and enlightens.[8]

I love the fact that in stating their education beliefs, they begin by talking about a "culture of achievement." In explaining their culture, the school's mission is very clear:

> Houston Arts Learning Academy has a liberal arts program. Of course we utilize our state curriculum which is the TEKS, but it is how we integrate the curriculum that ignites the learning. We use innovative techniques to teach and motivate students to venerate knowledge. Our curriculum is centered on integrated thematic units and experiential learning. The students receive a classical education that seamlessly builds their body of knowledge and skills from one year to the next which connect across grade levels and content areas. Additionally, the students are taught leadership and cooperative skills, through varied experiences which cultivate many facets of learning. We also utilize a Russian internet math program which instills a complete understanding of mathematics tailored to their specific needs for grades three through five. Additional web-based/white board programs are used to supplement our school wide math and reading programs for students in grades 2 through five. These programs offer instruction and reinforcement also in

the subjects of writing, and science. Sustaining the students interests through technological innovations is not the only way that we deepen the child's love for learning, we heavily rely on the tried and true methods of consistent high quality differentiated instruction, project based lessons, teacher collaboration and development, and parental involvement.

Passion, commitment, and implementation make the difference, it is our strength. We continuously look for ways to improve teaching skills so that the students will not just learn for the moment, but for a lifetime. Our team meets weekly to discuss the needs of the children from grade to grade as well as for advice and support for the classroom. Because we do not have extra staff, we all must be able to bear the weight of extra duties which only enhances our abilities to best serve the students. Additionally, we have developed professional learning communities with several traditional public and charter schools which enable us to collaborate on ideas that work best in the elementary science and math classroom to produce proficient young scientists, and or mathematicians. The administration also searches for teacher development opportunities with research proven results that are truly meaningful to the teacher which proves to enhance student's development as well utilizing the school motto "changing for the better."[9]

I also like the fact that the school is committed to making sure that each student becomes proficient in analytical thinking, something often missed with some "drill and kill" standardized test preparation approaches.

In all subjects, we use elaborative interrogations to make sure all vocabulary is understood. This promotes critical thinking and ensuring that students understand the entire concept and not just individual word definitions. It simplifies generalizations and gives the teacher the opportunity to assess the reasoning behind the response which generates elaborate answers. It assists students with absorbing new knowledge and creates interaction.[10]

The leader who drives it all is Principal East, an exuberant, African-American woman with a happy and pleasant presence. When I asked her about her school's learning culture and how she was able to build it, she immediately began to talk about relationships. "You have to have a relationship with the children, the parents, and the teachers in order to build a culture of learning," she said. "That is the only way to get the buy-in you need. Once you have established those relationships, then there is enough trust for you to be their facilitator; their entree to learning and growth."

For Yvette East, none of this was easy. She became a teacher at HHLA in 2002 and was quickly accepted as a great teacher. However, when she was named the school's principal in 2005, many of the HHLA's majority Latino parents were vocally disappointed. A petition was even circulated calling for a Latino principal. While painful to her at first, the experience taught Yvette a valuable lesson, one she employs today in her management of the school: the power of listening.

"That whole experience taught me how to listen and observe, and to do so patiently. I listened to my Latino parents and remained consistent in my approach with their children. Over time, the trust was established and the relationships were sealed."

From HHLA's Latino parents, Yvette also learned that it was important to have those same relationships with many of her students' grandparents, uncles, and aunts. Often the entire extended family of her Latino students was intimately involved in the child's education.

Yvette uses this same family concept to develop the learning culture at her school.

"Every teacher at our school knows every student by name. Yes, we are small enough for that to be possible, but every teacher feels responsible for the learning experience of every child. We promote a strong feeling of family. We believe in the human side. I believe a lot in team building and the whole, 'we are all in this together approach.' Everyone at our school is there to grow and learn—even the teachers. We celebrate each other's growth. And we take the same approach in the classroom with our students. We do very well on standardized tests, but we don't focus on the tests. Rather, we celebrate growth. If a student who may have been two grades behind at the start of the year ends the year at or near grade level, we make a big deal out of that, even if the child doesn't pass the test. We make sure the student's work is acknowledged."

In focusing on providing a learning culture in family environment and supportive setting, Yvette, by the way, has a school full of children who test very well. And the school parents love her. As one Latino parent said to me during my visit of the school, "Our principal, Ms. East, is the very, very best." I agree.

The HHLA in Houston, Texas, is a public charter school that has created a culture of learning.

Village Leadership Academy

The Village Leadership Academy (VLA) is a private K-8 elementary school located in the heart of Chicago's west side. VLA was founded by the owners of It Takes A Village Early Learning Centers and served its first class of kindergarteners in the fall of 2007. The teaching staff of It Takes A Village Early Learning Centers received rave reviews for the solid academic program they provided their preschoolers and quickly learned that the students' neighborhood schools were not prepared to continue to challenge the preschool graduates. Many of the preschool graduates left the Early Learning Centers reading and completing math concepts that most students do not master until the first or second grade. The parents of the Early Learning Centers urged the owners of It Takes A Village to open a school where high expectations and a rigorous academic program would be the norm. The founding principal of VLA is educator Nakisha Hobbs, a pleasant hard-working woman who is completely committed to the learning potential of her students. And she has a winning smile. Under Nakisha's leadership, VLA has emerged as an integral part of the community where it is located in a relatively short period of time. The key is Nakisha. Nakisha was born in Chicago, but when she was eleven years old, she moved with her mother to Omaha, Nebraska. She was immediately struck by the resources that the children had at her Omaha school. And all those children were engaged and invested in learning. All of which was foreign to her based on her experience within the Chicago public schools.

Nakisha went on to get her college degree from the University of Illinois at Chicago and a masters at Roosevelt University. While in a PhD program, it struck her that she should start a school. For her, it was important that the children in her school be exposed to a learning energy more like what she experienced in Omaha rather than what she saw during her early education years in Chicago. Nakisha also believes that it is important to train our children to be future leaders starting in kindergarten. As a result, VLA emphasizes the need for its students to understand complex community issues and then helps them develop the leadership skills to address them. Here is the VLA school mission:

> Village Leadership Academy's highly skilled staff of educators engages students in deep exploration of relevant high interest content in math, science, reading, language arts, social science, physical development, health awareness, fine arts, world languages (Spanish), social emotional development, technology and leadership development. This content is clearly explained, illustrated, modeled, reinforced and mastered with structured, guided and independent practice. We provide a superior education, grounded in real world experiences that help our students develop knowledge, skills, productive habits and a critical intellect. The academy guides students in realizing their potential for academic excellence and supports them in gaining the skills necessary to transform and advance their community, nation, and world.[11]

VLA educated 162 students in 2014–15 school year, 69 percent African American, 4 percent Asian, 23 percent Hispanic and 1 percent white, with 90 percent of the children on free and reduced lunch.[12] But it is a private school. So somehow, each of the children's families must find a way to pay the school's $8,000 per year tuition. Even here, however, Nakisha tries to help. According to Nakisha, 70 percent of the students' tuition is paid for by way of fundraising.

In keeping with the VLA mission, the schools' instructional model is uniquely focused on social justice. Check out some of their featured curriculum:

Social Justice & Global Studies Curriculum

VLA utilizes global studies curriculum and a social justice teaching approach, to engage students in uncovering social, political and economic systems impacting their lives and the lives of others. The curriculum is broken into six areas: All About Me, Africa, Asia, Europe, Latin America and the United States. Students become more aware of patterns of injustice and ways oppressed communities have combatted past injustices in order to inform their efforts towards social change. The curriculum exceeds state standards and replaces traditional social studies curricula. It is further integrated into visual arts, science, and physical education programs in order to support the development of the whole child.

Youth Organizing: Grassroots Campaign Projects

Beginning at the kindergarten level, each classroom develops an ongoing service-learning project designed to reduce a societal problem affecting their community, nation or world. Through participation in Grassroots Campaign projects students gain practical leadership, develop skills as they learn to amplify their voice, demand accountability from influential forces, and work to reduce social barriers.

Culturally Relevant Arts Programming

VLA students have access to high quality, engaging extracurricular programs which are infused into the extended school day. Extracurricular activities include traditional music instruction, dance, African Drumming, Capoeira, Tabura, and Step Team. The goal of this programming is the development of positive social skills to prevent at-risk behavior.

World Scholars Program (WSP)

The World Scholars Program teaches global leadership development through a year-long academic and extracurricular exploration of the history and culture of the Community of Focus. The students focus on the historical and cultural appreciation of people of the world; critical analysis of global commonalities and differences; and a culminating cultural and educational excursion to the Community of Focus.[13]

Nakisha is a one-person army in involving parents and students on field trips, visits with political leaders, and thoughtful debates and discussions about critical issues of the day. Having met and spoken with many of the school's parents, I was impressed with how much many of them admitted to have learned about world issues just by supporting their child's progress at the school. One parent told me, "I now read the paper differently and understand the news better now that my son is at VLA."

When I asked Nakisha what made her school unique, here is what she said:

Our focus is on empowering individual children to transform our community. And while we promote individual success, our children, parents and VLA family at large understands that individual success is not enough; that our collective success is the key. As a result, we all support each other every step of the way and that's how we have built a learning culture. At our school, the most popular children are the ones who work the hardest—that's because of our culture.

And the school's academics are strong. In nearly every category, in every grade, VLA students score in the 90 or high-80 percentile on the basic required standardized tests.[14] But for the VLA family of students, teachers, parents, and supporters, the school is not focused on the tests. They are building responsible leaders for tomorrow who happen to love learning.

The VLA in Chicago, Illinois, is a private school that has created a culture of learning.

The Lindsay Unified School District

The Salemwood School, the HHLA, and the VLA are all schools that have established learning cultures that have engulfed their entire school communities. And these schools are not alone. There are hundreds of schools located throughout America in which the children are learning, growing, and thriving as they move from grade to grade. For years, reformers have been pointing to such individual schools as examples of what is possible. By the same token, those same reformers are quick to point out how hard it is to create a culture of learning in an entire school district. I have been at numerous conferences where I hear reformers say wistfully, "Boy, I wish we could replicate or build to scale what they do in you-name-it-school." Or, "Why can't such-and-such network add a school in another city?"

"Nonprofit networks of charter operators with top-flight schools—outfits like Uncommon, KIPP and Aspire Public Schools—have created only about 350 in the past decade, and required $500 million in philanthropic support," according to Thomas Toch, author of a study last year on many of the groups underwritten by the New Schools Venture Fund. He questioned whether successful charters could be "scaled up" without sacrificing quality and without heavy subsidies from private donors.

"It's easy to open schools, but it's very hard to open and sustain and to grow networks of very good schools," said Mr. Toch, a founder of the research group, Education Sector.[15] Mr. Toch is right. It is hard to open and sustain a large group of schools—especially when you try to do so from the top down. Though well intentioned, most reformers have relied on cookie cutter approaches that worked in one community and, according to their logic, should work in every community. Looking at New Orleans as an example, unless an organic learning culture is built within a given community from the bottom up, the educational success of the children will always be short term, fleeting, or subject to continual community opposition and random legislative fiat.

Even big city school superintendents bemoan the fact that the various oases of success that may exist in one part of the town are virtually impossible to replicate in the poorer areas of their respective district. Often, they point to poverty, work rules, and bad leadership as causes. In response, enterprising school superintendents work very hard to streamline their bureaucracies, give greater autonomy to their best principals, and encourage innovation in their schools. But even in those circumstances it is rare to see a concentrated effort to reconstruct a community-wide learning culture. That said, it can be done, and academic success can take place on a large scale in a way to allow personalized learning to thrive. And it is being done in the rural, poverty-stricken Californian school district known as Lindsay Unified.

* * *

Nine in a row was just too much. Much too much. For Tom Rooney and his colleagues, that is when the seeds of change began—when they realized that nine consecutive Lindsay Unified School District (LUSD) high-school valedictorians all had to take remedial courses in college. Nine straight. Lindsay's very best students were not ready for college.

Of course, there were other signs. Like when the father of a recent graduate marched into the high-school principal's office with his son, held a newspaper in front of his son, and told him to read it to the principal.

"Dad, you know I can't read," the son told the father. The father got up to leave, looked at the principal, and said sarcastically, "Your graduate."

As shocking as stories like these were, it was easy to attribute Lindsay students' lack of proficiency to their environment. Lindsay, California, is nestled at the base of the Sierra Nevadas in the San Joaquin Valley nearly halfway between Bakersfield and Fresno, the heart of migrant worker land. Lindsay is full of orange groves, dusty rolling hills, and the famous Lindsay olives. It also boasts some of the poorest demographics in the country. This town of just under 12,000 people is 85 percent Hispanic and half of families make less than $35,000 per year, according to census data.[16] But that is merely what is reported. Many Lindsay residents are undocumented and are barely making ends meet. According to officials at the Lindsay School District, 43 percent of parents in the Lindsay district do not have a high-school education, and as of the fall of 2015, 87 percent of the students are on the federally funded free or reduced lunch program. As one Lindsay school administrator told me, "We would love to be able to say that our parents are in the working class. In fact, that would be a dream."

As is the case in any low-income, economically challenged community, rampant poverty brings with it a host of other problems. Drugs, gangs, shootings, alcohol abuse, and other social maladies were part of everyday life in Lindsay, and much of it bled into the schools. There were artificial boundaries on the high-school playground in red and blue, marking the gang territories; a major fight occurred on school property nearly every day; suspensions and expulsions were commonplace. Teachers and administrators did what they could to maintain order, but under these circumstances, it was hard for learning to take place for most of the four thousand plus students enrolled in LUSD. Why expect more, right?

Still, what about the best of the best? That's what initially gnawed at Rooney. What does it say about an entire school district when even the best students are not learning? In 2007, then Lindsay Superintendent Janet Kliegl and Assistant Superintendent for Curriculum and Instruction Tom Rooney faced those questions head on. Rooney began to ask himself more questions about the value of learning and why he and his colleagues do what they do. In his own mind, he questioned the basics. What if learning could happen anytime, anywhere, and could be about anything? What if learning were recognized as a lifelong endeavor? What if learning could be engaging, inspiring, relevant, and gasp, fun? Even in Lindsay?

Working with their fellow administrators, teachers, and school board members, Kliegl and Rooney openly and critically faced the facts in front of them: Lindsay students were bored, disconnected, and frustrated; teachers were burned out and uninspired; few students were learning in LUSD. They then made a conscious decision to throw out everything that they had done in past. Everything. And they then started again from scratch. The school leadership team realized that they needed to build a learning culture. But they also realized that the building of that culture could not be done in a top-down manner, especially not in Lindsay, California. So they did something that, as far as I know, no other school district in America has done: they decided to involve the entire Lindsay community in redesigning education and learning for LUSD. From the very beginning of the process.

In January 2007, Lindsay held the first of several community meetings to discuss how to reshape learning in their community. Hundreds attended the initial meeting. The district recognized that they needed a set of principles that would guide its redesign. They also knew that the community needed to develop those principles. This recognition has been key to Lindsay's transformation and success. In most places, the so-called experts develop a strategic plan and then present it to selected stakeholders for little, if any, opportunity for change. In Lindsay, at the start of the process, everyone was invited to participate and weigh in.

At the first meeting, a facilitator helped guide the process. The leadership outlined everything from why they exist as an organization to how they believe students learn best and even included a description of what a Lindsay graduate looks like. The following questions helped jump start the process:

- Why do we exist as an organization?
- What are the values that will govern how we act toward one another?
- What are the principles by which we will make decisions?
- What is our vision for the future with regard to learning, instruction, curriculum, assessment, technology, leadership, personnel, and stakeholders?
- What is the description of our graduate?

Follow-up community meetings took place for several months. From May through late July 2007, Lindsay community groups met to discuss and refine the work that was completed at a special May 2007 community forum. All participants stripped themselves of their own preconceived notions of what education should be. Many of the participants of those sessions wistfully recall the countless "what if" questions that were, for the first time, honestly considered by the group. They also remember the liberating feeling that came with answering those "what if" questions without the shackles of the old system holding them back. These engaged diverse voices—educators, principals, district leaders, parents, union leaders, city officials, and community members—created a new vision of learning for Lindsay, California. Thousands of Lindsay residents offered feedback, as did each stakeholder. At the core of this new approach was culture. As Tom Rooney says, "we knew we could not create a set of principles in a vacuum. We had to create a new culture of learning for everyone. That culture had to be saturated throughout Lindsay."

From those initial questions, the voice of the community collectively created the Lindsay Unified Strategic Design which essentially defines Lindsay's Mission, Core Values, Guiding Principles, Vision for the Future, and Lifelong Learning Standards.[17]

After several iterations and additional community feedback over the course of three months, the strategic design was formally adopted by the local school board and became the guiding document that led Lindsay toward building a personalized learning system throughout the district (referred to now as the LUSD Performance-Based System). Consistent with the community engagement approach taken by school officials from the beginning of the process, the final plans were spread throughout the district, in a small church-like pamphlet, written in clear language for everyone to understand and own.

It would be an understatement to call the ultimate plan that Lindsay adopted radical. And yet, after nearly ten years, it works for kids and has transformed Lindsay into a true learning culture. The essence of the Lindsay plan is that the entire school district is a totally customized system where personalized learning is in place for each and every student. As I was told numerous times during my visit, the Lindsay approach is not a pilot, it is who they are. They have adopted a complete competency-based personalized learning model.

For Lindsay, that means that students are grouped by content levels, which correlate to grade levels based on what part of state-level curriculum students should be learning in that grade. A thirteen-year-old who would normally be in eighth grade, for example, could be in seventh-grade content-level math or ninth-grade content-level English or stay in the eighth-grade content level for all subjects, among other combinations.

Students stair-step from one lesson to the next throughout the school year based on how quickly they can prove to their teachers they know individual concepts.

They do so by writing papers, completing projects, filling out worksheets, and taking tests. Only when an assignment is completed satisfactorily can a student move on to the next concept in the syllabus. Lindsay expects students to demonstrate mastery of a subject before they can move on.

As part of the redesign, Lindsay scrapped the traditional alphabetic grading system and replaced it with a scoring scale tied to specific standards of learning. That's right. There are no grades given in LUSD. As Tom Rooney explains, "In Lindsay, in the past we had too many learners pushed through a time-based system with C's or D's or A's that were faked and we sent them off. Today we are responsible for every student in our system—they need to be ready for what comes next."

To get their students ready for the change, Lindsay officials defined the key participants differently. Lindsay students are referred to as learners, not students, while teachers are called "learning facilitators." The leadership then placed greater emphasis on ensuring that learners "know the subject that they were studying" and they adopted a rating system to gauge a learner's knowledge. To receive the highest rating of "4" on a particular topic, students must, at their own direction, go beyond what they've learned in class to apply the knowledge and skills in a new context. Students receive a "3" if they master complex and simple skills, a "2" if they master simple skills only, and a "1" if they master simple skills with help. All students must achieve at least a "3" to progress to their next learning target.

As hard as it is to implement, the personalized learning approach really makes more sense for many of today's children, particularly in view of the diverse needs of our students. And for those students who may be further behind, the no grades/no labels concept frees them to learn without the stigma of being dumb or slow. I visited several Lindsay schools and talked with students in various classrooms. It was inspiring to see fourth graders sitting and learning math on their own computer and sharing their progress with each other as their learning facilitator could be found nearby, monitoring the various groups and ready to answer specific learners' questions. Or the seventh graders who told me how they were able to balance working alone or with a group without the worry of being distracted. And I was so impressed with the high schoolers who showed me how they stayed on top of their history assignments through use of their learning targets and goals sheet. And all students were moving at their own pace. In speaking with several learning facilitators, I hear countless success stories about learners who, but for this approach, would have been lost. Like the boy who immigrated to Lindsay from Mexico at fourteen unable to speak any English. He had entered the United States by being thrown over a fence at the border and when he arrived in Lindsay, he was academically lost. A personalized plan was constructed for this boy, who did not have to worry about being graded. He quickly thrived and a love of learning kicked in. He especially loved writing and within a couple of years, he was fluent enough in English to be able to write a book about his personal immigration experience. He even had a book party at his school where he wore a borrowed suit. The young man graduated from high school, went to a local community college, and then to Fresno State, where he is majoring in English. He plans on returning to Lindsay so he can teach English at LUSD.

I also heard about the "5th grade genius learner." This boy was so advanced that he was academically ready for high school when he was in the fifth grade. He was not, however, socially ready to be in a high-school setting with learners as old as eighteen years of age. Consistent with the model, the Lindsay team structured a learning schedule for him so that he could remain in his classroom. This unique and personalized schedule allowed him to go to the high school first thing in the morning for special algebra instruction with a high-school math teacher before joining his fifth-grade classmates back at his elementary school by the second period. Since they began this approach, Lindsay officials are adamant about meeting each and every learner "where they actually are, as opposed to where we think they should be."

In addition to the academic support, the fifth-grade genius story illuminates another key component of the Lindsay Strategic Design. LUSD strongly believes in educating the whole child. To do so, district leaders place a significant emphasis on each learner's social development and social services needs. I was told by several teachers and administrators of examples in which learners were not promoted because they were not socially ready to go to the next grade, even though they were academically ready to be promoted. Lindsay officials have a deep commitment to the social development of their learners so that they enter the world fully prepared to be productive. To that end, the district has a site-based Family Resource Center at one of the schools that is fully staffed with social workers, nurses, case managers, and substance abuse counselors. This kind of support is critical in a school district with such entrenched poverty and dysfunctional family settings. For instance, I was also told that as of early 2016, over five hundred of the LUSD students were homeless. All of them receive support from the school beyond the school day, which officially runs from 8 AM to 3 PM After school, however, from 3 PM to 6 PM, a full range of mentoring and after-school care is provided, a service also used by most students. As part of their commitment to educate the whole child, district support staff is kept apprised of issues or challenges involving the learners. It is not unusual for schools in Lindsay to have meetings with classified staff members, namely maintenance and operations staff, classroom aides, and food service staff, among others, to discuss the classroom activities and specific social challenges that impact individual learners. If you are in that child's orbit, you play an integral role in the child's ability to succeed, so by definition, you are in the loop—you are on the team.

Of course, technology is a big part of the new Lindsay learning model. All of the four thousand plus LUSD learners have their own personal computers or, in the case of young learners, tablets. In late 2015, LUSD began to provide WiFi connections for the homes of every learner. As they embarked on the task of wiring their learners' homes, the LUSD technology team realized that there was a challenge accessing some of the more rural houses. This is where the years' long community engagement paid off. LUSD was able to attach a router on every tenth home throughout the district, which led to full computer access for every student. They did so without any complaints from the non-LUSD households they approached about installing the routers. Lindsay officials continue to engage the community through periodic meetings and updates. Virtually every community contact is grass roots in nature, and great pains are taken to ensure that no one is left out.

So how effective has the Lindsay design been?

In 2009, only 25 percent of students were proficient in reading and only 28 percent in math. The academic gains since then have been modest. But, as was highlighted in an Ed Surge article which chronicled the Lindsay experience, success cannot be viewed from the test scores lens alone.

> Since 2009, scores have risen incrementally. The district has seen a 9 percent increase in the number of students (grades two to 11) rated "proficient" in English language arts (from 25 percent to 34 percent), a 4 percent increase in math (from 28 percent to 32 percent), and 14 percent rise in science (from 27 percent to 41 percent). Scores on the state's Academic Performance Index (API) have also made modest gains, rising from 644 in 2009 to 691 in 2013.

> While the gain on the API outperforms the state average increase of 35-points, Lindsay's overall proficiency scores are still well below the state average. In California, average proficiency in math was 51 percent in 2013. In English language arts that average was 56 percent.

> But test scores might not be the best metric by which to measure Lindsay's success. Because the state requires districts to test students at the level associated with their age, and not their abilities, the scores on state tests don't entirely reflect the level a student is working at. For instance, a 13-year-old student might have completed 80 percent of the content in 6th grade. However, she must still take the test for 8th graders.

> [. . .]

> However, the district is seeing gains in other areas of school culture. Since implementation of the new model, suspension rates have dropped by 41 percent and gang membership has fallen from 18 percent to 3 percent. District officials see these metrics as indicators that students see school as a place for opportunity, support, and hope.

> Whatever the results, dismantling a 150-year old system isn't easy. But students seem to be embracing their new opportunities, and embodying a new way of looking at their growth.

> "It used to be all about the teacher. Now it's all about us," says one 13-year old Lindsay "learner."[18]

It is also noteworthy that more Lindsay learners are going to college. According to Lindsay officials, in 2009, only 20 percent of Lindsay high-school graduates enrolled in a four-year college. As of 2015, that number increased to 41 percent. (Incidentally, Lindsay officials maintain that the no-grades approach has had no negative effect on college access.)

Tom Rooney continues to drive the changes at LUSD. In 2012, he became the LUSD superintendent and he remains steadfast in his commitment to the Lindsay Strategic Design. Now that he has total community buy-in, he wants to drill down even more on the academics. Implementing the competency-based personalized learning model is hard, especially on the teachers. Rooney has had to deal with a fair amount of turnover, but he and his team have begun to realize that hiring the right people and asking the right questions during the hiring process is key. Nikolaus Namba is the principal of Kennedy Elementary located in the LUSD. Principal Namba has spent his entire career working in competency-based systems in places like Denver, Colorado, and Los Angeles, California. When we talked, Principal Namba told me that it all comes down to culture. "Culture is essential," he said. "And everyone I hire has to buy into the culture. During the interview process, I have learned not to ask about qualifications, skill-set or views on curriculum. I start with their mindset. I need to see and feel my potential teachers' hearts. I need to know that they believe that all kids can learn and that they believe in the model. Once I know that they have bought into our culture of learning and our guiding principles, then we can move on with the process."

Great things are happening in Lindsay. But, according to Superintendent Rooney, the best is yet to come. He insists, "We are not just reforming education, we are completely dismantling the traditional time-based structures and building a learner-centered system of empowerment."

The LUSD in Lindsay, California, is a school district that has created a culture of learning.

We should be informed and encouraged by the learning cultures we see at the Salemwood School, the HHLA, the Village Learning Academy, and the LUSD. It can be done, but time is of the essence. Coming together to build a learning culture throughout America should be our new national imperative.

During my visits to each of these schools—and others like them—I intuitively could tell that a culture of learning was abound. The learning culture that has been established at each of these schools has trickled into their surrounding communities. And it is not based on test scores or awards; it is based on the holistic approach taken by the school leaders, their administrators, staff, and teachers. The children in these schools believe they can learn, they have fun learning, and their experiences have become positively infectious for the whole community.

Many American schools work for our children. There is no one cookie-cutter way to make a school work. Each of the schools you just read about emerged from different educational systems or providers and they each employ uniquely different approaches. But they all work well for children and each was built organically, from the bottom up, in a way that ensured that their learning message would extend beyond their school doors. America needs to know about these schools. We need to cherish them and provide ways for them to share their approaches so others can emulate them. More and more emphasis must be placed on using these schools, and others like them, as symbols of excellence. These symbols must not be tied to test scores or short-term learning that is here today, gone tomorrow. I envision using the trusted voices and influencers mentioned previously as a way to broadcast, amplify, and ultimately multiply the outputs we see from the schools that work, be they traditional public, public charter, private, or any other school with a true learning culture. Individuals need to know that great schools that are "Made in America" can exist anywhere in America.

Notes

1. Salemwood Elementary School, Public School Review Online, accessed January 4, 2016, http://www.publicschoolreview.com/salemwood-elementary-school-profile.
2. Stacy Teicher Khadaroo, "How One Massachusetts Town Turned around Early Reading Program," The Christian Science Monitor Online, May 26, 2015, http://www.csmonitor.com/USA/Education/2015/0526/How-one-Massachusetts-town-turned-around-early-reading-program.
3. "Malden Public Schools Mission & Vision," Salemwood School, accessed January 4, 2016, http://maldenps.org/salemwood/about/general-information/unique-featuresdescription-and-unique-features-description-

and-unique-features-ms-keenan-principal-ckeenanmalden-mec-edu-k-4-office-781-3/.

4. "2012 Accountability Data—Malden," Massachusetts Department of Elementary and Secondary Education, accessed January 4, 2016, http:// profiles.doe.mass.edu/accountability/report/district.aspx?orgtypecode= 5&linkid=30&fycode=2012&orgcode=01650000.

5. "Our Mission," Houston Heights Learning Academy Website, accessed January 4, 2016, http://www.heightslearning.org/apps/pages/index.jsp? uREC_ID=215004&type=d&pREC_ID=475320.

6. Houston Heights Learning Academy, Public School Review, accessed January 4, 2016, http://www.publicschoolreview.com/houston-heights-learning-academy-inc-profile.

7. Houston Heights Learning Academy, Trulia, accessed January 4, 2016, http://www.trulia.com/school-district/TX-Harris_County/Houston_Heights_Learning_Academy_Inc/.

8. "Beliefs and Visions: Education Beliefs," Houston Heights Learning Academy, accessed January 24, 2016, http://www.heightslearning.org/apps/ pages/index.jsp?uREC_ID=215004&type=d&pREC_ID=475282.

9. Houston Heights Learning Academy, National Title I Association, accessed January 4, 2016, http://www.titlei.org/ds/schools/houston-heights-learning-academy.

10. Houston Heights Learning Academy, National Title I Association, accessed January 4, 2016, http://www.titlei.org/ds/schools/houston-heights-learning-academy.

11. "Mission," Village Leadership Academy, accessed January 4, 2016, http:// www.vlacademy.org/about-village-leadership-academy/missionvision/.

12. "2014 Illinois School Report Cards: Village Leadership Academy,"*Chicago Tribune*, accessed January 4, 2016, http://schools.chicagotribune.com/ school/village-leadership-academy_chicago.

13. "Instructional Model," Village Leadership Academy, accessed January 4, 2016, http://www.vlacademy.org/instructional-model/.

14. "2014 Illinois School Report Cards: Village Leadership Academy," *Chicago Tribune*, accessed January 4, 2016, http://schools.chicagotribune.com/ school/village-leadership-academy_chicago.

15. Trip Gabriel, "Despite Push, Success at Charter Schools Is Mixed," *The New York Times* Online, May 1, 2010, http://www.nytimes.com/2010/05/02/ education/02charters.html?pagewanted=all&_r=1.

16. Lindsay, CA Population: 2010 Census, accessed January 24, 2016, http:// censusviewer.com/city/CA/Lindsay.

17. The Lindsay Unified Strategic Design can be found at http://www.lindsay. k12.ca.us/filelibrary/LUSD%20Strategic%20Design%201.pdf.

- Mission—Empowering and Motivating for Today and Tomorrow.
- Core Values—Guide our behavior; govern how we will work together as we carry out the mission and vision and include integrity, commitment, excellence, risk-taking, teamwork, accountability, improvement, openness, alignment, and courage.
- Guiding Principles.

- Vision for the Future.
- Lifelong Learning Standards.

18. Christina Quattrocchi, "How Lindsay Unified Redesigned Itself from the Ground Up," *edSurge*, June 17, 2014, https://cedsurge.herokuapp. com/news/2014-06-17-how-lindsay-unified-redesigned-itself-from-the-ground-up.

Conclusion: Finding Hope

Just before America entered World War II, Great Britain was in near total distress. Hitler's German troops were steadily bombing the once mighty nation and British citizens experienced a growing acceptance of the inevitability of falling under Nazi rule. The country had lost its confidence, its spirit, and its fight—all except its prime minister, Winston Churchill. Diminutive in stature, yet bombastic in bearing, Churchill easily took over each room that he entered. He naturally oozed leadership, and his confidence was unshakable. He was the perfect leader at the right time for England.

As the backs of many of his fellow countrymen began to bend, Churchill stood tall, all 5'6" of him. Known for pounding the podium while boldly cajoling those he served to never give in, he was able to tap into one of the essential drivers of human existence: *hope*. Churchill reminded Britain that "success is not final, failure is not fatal: it is the courage to continue that counts" and thereby inspired a whole nation that its brightest days extended beyond Hitler's bombs. In effect, Churchill was telling his fellow Brits that vision is seeing beyond what you can see. That inspiration helped steer the way toward winning the Great War.

In many ways, Churchill's spirit can be appropriately applied to the future of learning in America. On the brave new road to customized and lifelong learning, we don't know for certain what the future holds, but we do know that it has the potential to revolutionize our world. We just need to believe that it will. And in the process, let's inspire our children to believe it as well.

Years ago, after speaking in Little Rock, Arkansas, I visited a charter school outside of the city. The school was located literally "on the other side of the tracks" where most of the citizens were African American and extremely poor. I had recently left public office in DC and was just beginning my work as a national advocate

187

for educational choice. This particular kindergarten to eighth grade school was getting amazing results from their children and I was eager to visit with the teachers and students.

As I was parking my rental car, I noticed that the school consisted of a row of trailers positioned around an old parking lot. It looked different from any school that I had ever visited. I was greeted with an exuberant smile from the school founder, who led me on my tour. As we walked from trailer to trailer, the poverty jumped out at me. Many of the children, and even some teachers, had old or tattered clothes. A few of the children were barefoot. Yet each person I met was smiling and happy, teachers and students alike. But more than anything, I was struck by the learning taking place in the school. Kindergartners and first graders were on computers, second graders joyfully read to me, and sixth graders couldn't wait to show me their science projects. Every face I saw was full of excitement, enthusiasm, and hope. When I walked into one classroom, a couple of the young boys excitedly asked if they could tell me about the books they were reading. That moment, the look in their faces reminded me of me. That little boy, growing up in Indianapolis, eagerly waiting to tell his father about the book he just finished reading. The young boy, Kevin, who enjoyed learning.

Since that day, I have visited hundreds of schools around the country where the same energy exists, schools that are getting incredible results and outputs as a result of their ability to inspire children to want to learn. But I have never, before or since, been in a school which contained so much laughter, so much *joy* around learning. It was truly a spiritual experience.

For me, that school visit brought Churchill's words to life. The future of those children, in that Little Rock school, even the poorest and shoeless among them, would not be dictated by the social circumstances of their birth. Rather the future for those children would be dictated by their continued enthusiasm for learning and growing. Their future, their vision, would extend beyond what even I could see on that day. And just the thought of that school visit continues to make me smile.

Given the chance, all American children can enjoy their schooling just like those children I saw that day in Little Rock. That is my hope. That is my vision. Ultimately, our societal evolution will be guided by citizens who fully understand and appreciate the value of learning and by our ability to continually foster curiosity and a quest for knowledge in each and every one of our children. While no one can say for sure where such a commitment to learning will lead our nation or our world, I do know that in our new learning culture, our brightest days are yet to come.

Bibliography

AFC Policy Summit - Mike McCurry, posted by American Federation for Children on May 21, 2013, https://www.youtube.com/watch?v=MnUaIMexGxc&feature=youtu.be&noredirect=1.

Anderson, James D. *The Education of Blacks in the South 1860–1935*. Chapel Hill: The University of North Carolina Press, 1988.

Anderson, Nick. "Education Secretary Duncan Calls Hurricane Katrina Good for New Orleans Schools." *The Washington Post Online*, January 30, 2010, http://www.washingtonpost.com/wp-dyn/content/article/2010/01/29/AR2010012903259.html.

Atkin, S. Beth. *Voices from the Fields: Children of Migrant Farmworkers Tell Their Stories*. Boston, MA: Little, Brown, and Company, 1993.

Babcock, Elisabeth D. "Rethinking Poverty." *Stanford Social Innovation Review*, Fall 2014, http://www.liveworkthrive.org/site/assets/docs/SSIR_Fall_2014_Rethinking_Poverty.pdf.

Babcock, Elisabeth D. *Using Brain Science to Design New Pathways Out of Poverty*, Crittenton Women's Union, 2014, http://www.liveworkthrive.org/site/assets/Using%20Brain%20Science%20to%20Create%20Pathways%20Out%20of%20Poverty%20FINAL%20online.pdf.

Beliefs and Visions: Education Beliefs. Houston Heights Learning Academy, Accessed January 24, 2016. http://www.heightslearning.org/apps/pages/index.jsp?uREC_ID=215004&type=d&pREC_ID=475282.

Berwick, Carly. "The Great German School Turnaround." *The Atlantic Online*, November 3, 2015. http://www.theatlantic.com/education/archive/2015/11/great-german-scool-turnaround/413806/.

Branch, Taylor. *Parting the Waters: America in the King Years 1954–63*. New York: Simon & Schuster, 1988.

A Brief Overview of Progressive Education, The Dewey Project on Progressive Education at University of Vermont. Accessed December 29, 2015. http://www.uvm.edu/~dewey/articles/proged.html.

Brill, Steven. *Class Warfare: Inside the Fight to Fix America's Schools*. New York: Simon & Schuster, 2011.

Brown at 60: The Southern Manifesto and "Massive Resistance" to Brown. NAACP Legal Defense and Educational Fund. Accessed December 29, 2015. http://www.naacpldf.org/brown-at-60-southern-manifesto-and-massive-resistance-brown.

Brown, Richard D. *The Strength of a People: The Idea of an Informed Citizenry in America, 1650–1870*. Chapel Hill: University of North Carolina Press, 2010.

Brown v. Board of Education of Topeka, 347 U.S. 483 (1954).

Budde, Ray. *Education by Charter: Redistricting School Districts.* Andover, MA: The Regional Laboratory for Educational Improvement of the Northeast & Islands, 1988. https://www.edreform.com/wp-content/uploads/2014/12/Education-by-Charter-Restructuring-School-Districts-Ray-Budde.pdf.

Budget History Tables, Education Department Budget History Table: FY 1980— FY 2016 President's Budget. U.S. Department of Education Online. Accessed December 29, 2015. http://www2.ed.gov/about/overview/budget/history/index.html.

Burke, Lindsay, and Rachel Sheffield. *School Choice in America 2011: Educational Opportunity Reaches New Heights.* The Heritage Foundation. http://www.heritage.org/research/reports/2011/08/school-choice-in-america-2011-educational-opportunity-reaches-new-heights.

Butcher, Jonathan. June 17, 2015, *Nevada's Education Gambit,* US News. http://www.usnews.com/opinion/knowledge-bank/2015/06/17/nevadas-new-education-savings-accounts-will-give-parents-lots-of-options.

Canada, Geoffrey. *Foreword: Voices of Determination* by Kevin P Chavous. New Brunswick, NJ: Transaction Publishers, 2012.

Caplan, Nathan, John K. Whitmore, and Marcella H. Choy. *The Boat People and Achievement in America: A Study of Economic and Educational Success.* Ann Arbor: The University of Michigan Press, 1989.

The Case against Vouchers, National Education Association. Accessed December 30, 2015. http://www.nea.org/home/19133.htm.

Charter Schools: Finding Out the Facts: At a Glance, Charter Schools Across the Nation. Center for Public Education. Accessed January 2, 2016. http://www.centerforpubliceducation.org/Main-Menu/Organizing-a-school/Charter-schools-Finding-out-the-facts-At-a-glance#sthash. PbH43442.dpuf.

Chartier, Michael. *Everything You Need to Know about Nevada's Universal ESA Bill.* Friedman Foundation for Educational Choice. Accessed January 2, 2016. http://www.edchoice.org/everything-you-need-to-know-about-nevadas-universal-esa-bill/.

Chavous, Kevin. Speech given at the School Choice Week Rally in Birmingham, Alabama, January 22, 2014.

Chavous, Kevin. *Voices of Determination: Children that Defy the Odds.* New Brunswick: Transaction Publishers, 2012.

Chavous, Kevin P. *Serving Our Children: Charter Schools and the Reform of American Public Education.* Herndon, VA: Capital Books, 2004.

Chavous, Kevin P. *This Toxic Standards Fight Isn't Helping Students,* Education Week, April 11, 2014. http://www.edweek.org/ew/articles/2014/04/11/28chavous.h33.html.

Coyne, Tom. *Indiana Public Schools Wage Unusual Ad Campaign to Keep Students from Leaving for Private Schools in Voucher Program.* The Huffington Post, August 20, 2012, http://www.huffingtonpost.com/2012/08/20/indiana-public-schools-wa_0_n_1813143.html.

Cremin, Lawrence A. *The Republic and the School: Horace Mann on the Education of Free Men.* New York: Teachers College, 1957.

Crosby, Brian. *The $100,000 Teacher: A Teacher's Solution to America's Declining Public School System.* Sterling: Capital Books, 2002.

Cubberley, Ellwood P. *Public Education in the United States.* Cambridge: Houghton Mifflin, 1919.

DC's Public Charter Schools: Reform that Works for DC's Most Underserved Children. FOCUS.Accessed December 30, 2015. http://www.focusdc.org/charter-facts.

DeBonis, Mike. "Fishing for DCPS Students."*The Washington Post Online,* July 2, 2014. https://www.washingtonpost.com/blogs/mike-debonis/wp/2014/07/02/fishing-for-dcps-students/.

Detroit Has Worst High School Graduation Rate, NPR, June 29, 2007. http://www.npr.org/templates/story/story.php?storyId=11601692.

Diperna, Paul. 2015 Schooling in America Survey. Friedman Foundation for Educational Choice, posted June 30, 2015. http://www.edchoice.org/research/2015-schooling-in-america-survey/; http://www.edchoice.org/research/school-choice-and-economic-growth/.

Duncan, Cynthia M. *Worlds Apart: Why Poverty Persists in Rural America.* New Haven, CT: Yale University Press, 1999.

Earth Day: History of a Movement. Earth Day Network. Accessed January 2, 2016. http://www.earthday.org/earth-day-history-movement.

The Economic Impact of the Achievement Gap in America's Schools. McKinsey & Company: Social Sector Office, April 2009. http://mckinseyonsociety.com/downloads/reports/Education/achievement_gap_report.pdf.

ED IN 08 Unveils New Analysis and Report Card Surrounding 25th Anniversary of a Nation at Risk. Strong American Schools Online Archive. Accessed December 29, 2015. https://web.archive.org/web/20080828192156/http://www.edin08.com/uploadedFiles/Issues/A%20Stagnant%20Nation.pdf.

Educational Reforms from the Early 1900's. Beavercreek Schools Unofficial Web Page. Accessed December 29, 2015. http://personalweb.donet.com/~eprice/fare.htm#nmsaovrv.

The Elements of Change: The Education Trust 2013 Annual Report. Accessed January 2, 2016. http://2013annualreport.edtrust.org.

Equiano, Olaudah. *The Interesting Narrative of the Life of Olaudah Equiano, Or Gustavus Vassa, the African,* 88, London, Ninth Edition enlarged, 1794.

Facts and Figures: Background and Trends. DC Public Charter School Board. Accessed December 28, 2016. http://www.dcpcsb.org/facts-and-figures.

Florida's Tax Credit Scholarship Program Participation. Friedman Foundation for Education Choice. Accessed January 2, 2016. http://www.edchoice.org/school-choice/programs/Florida-Tax-Credit-Scholarship-Program/.

Gabriel, Trip. "Despite Push, Success at Charter Schools Is Mixed."*New York Times Online,* May 1, 2010. http://www.nytimes.com/2010/05/02/education/02charters.html?pagewanted=all&_r=1.

*Germany: Key Findings, PISA Results from PISA 2012, OECD 2012.*Accessed January 2, 2016. http://www.oecd.org/pisa/keyfindings/PISA-2012-results-germany.pdf, 1.

Germany: Once Weak International Standing Prompts Strong Nation-wide Reforms for Rapid Improvement, Strong Performers and Successful Reformers in Education: Lessons from PiSA for the United States. OECD 2010. Accessed January 2, 2016. http://www.oecd.org/pisa/pisaproducts/46581323.pdf.

Global Consumers Vote Al Gore, Oprah Winfrey and Kofi Annan Most Influential to Champion Global Warming Cause: A Nielsen Survey, Market Research World. July 7, 2007. http://www.marketresearchworld.net/content/view/1394/77/.

Goldin, Claudia. "The Human-Capital Century and American Leadership: Virtues of the Past."*Journal of Economic History* 61, no. 2 (2001): 263–92.

Goldin, Claudia and Lawrence F. Katz. "Human Capital and Social Capital: The Rise of Secondary Schooling in America, 1910–1940." *Journal of Interdisciplinary History* 29, no. 4(1999): 683–723.

The Greatest Speech Ever – Robert F Kennedy Announcing The Death of Martin Luther King. Posted by Mohammad Azzam, posted on January 4, 2013. https://www.youtube.com/watch?v=GoKzCff8Zbs.

Griffin et al. v. County School Board of Prince Edward County et al., 377 U.S. 218 (1964).

Griswold, Eliza. *How "'Silent Spring' Ignited the Environmental Movement."The New York Times Online,* September 21, 2012. http://www.nytimes.com/2012/09/23/magazine/how-silent-spring-ignited-the-environmental-movement.html.

Hampton, Henry. *Eyes on the Prize: America's Civil Rights Years 1954–1965.* Arlington, VA: PBS, 1987–1990.

Hannah-Jones, Nikole. "A Prescription for More Black Doctors."*New York Times Online,* September 9, 2015. http://www.nytimes.com/2015/09/13/magazine/a-prescription-for-more-black-doctors.html.

Hayes, William. *Horace Mann's Vision of the Public Schools: Is it Still Relevant?* Lanham, MD: Rowman & Littlefield Education, 2006.

Hearing, Before the Subcommittee on the District of Columbia of the Committee on Government Reform and Oversight House of Representatives One Hundred Fifth Congress Second Session. Accessed December 29, 2015. http://files.eric.ed.gov/fulltext/ED425615.pdf.

Hess, Frederick M. *Cage-Busting Leadership.* Cambridge, MA: Harvard Education Press, 2013.

Historical Enrollment – Public Schools: 1967–2015 Public School Enrollment in the District. DC Public Charter School Board. Accessed January 2, 2016. https://data.dcpcsb.org/Enrollment-/Historial-Enrollment-Public-Schools/3db5-ujzr.

History, American Federation of Teachers. Accessed January 2, 2016. http://www.aft.org/about/history.

The History Behind the Little Rock Nine. State of Arkansas Official Website. Accessed December 29, 2015. http://www.arkansas.com/attractions/central-high/.

Houston Heights Learning Academy. National Title I Association. Accessed January 4, 2016. http://www.titlei.org/ds/schools/houston-heights-learning-academy.

Houston Heights Learning Academy. Public School Review. Accessed January 4, 2016. http://www.publicschoolreview.com/houston-heights-learning-academy-inc-profile.

Houston Heights Learning Academy. Trulia. Accessed January 4, 2016. http://www.trulia.com/school-district/TX-Harris_County/Houston_Heights_Learning_Academy_Inc/.

Howell, Mark C. "John Ben Shepperd, Attorney General of the State of Texas: His Role in the Continuation of Segregation in Texas, 1953–1957." Master's Thesis, The University of Texas of the Permian Basin, Odessa, Texas, July 2003.

Hsu, Spenser S. *How Vouchers Came to D.C.*EducationNext, Fall 2004, Vol 4, no. 4. http://educationnext.org/howvoucherscametodc/.

Hunter, John. *Teaching with the World Peace Game.* TED Talks TED2011. March 2011.Accessed January 4, 2016. https://www.ted.com/talks/john_hunter_on_ the_world_peace_game?language=en.

Hunter, John and Chris Farina. *World Peace and other 4th Grade Achievements.* Charlottesville, VA: Silverthorn Films, 2014.

In Praise of the Counterculture. The New York Times Online. December 11, 1994. http://www.nytimes.com/1994/12/11/opinion/in-praise-of-the-coun-terculture.html.

Ingraham, Christopher. "Charting the Shocking Rise of Racial Disparity in Our Criminal Justice System."*the Washington Post Online,* July 15, 2014. https://www.washingtonpost.com/news/wonk/wp/2014/07/15/charting-the-shock-ing-rise-of-racial-disparity-in-our-criminal-justice-system/.

Instructional Model. Village Leadership Academy. Accessed January 4, 2016. http://www.vlacademy.org/instructional-model/.

Interposition Resolution by the Florida Legislature in Response to Brown v. Board of Education, 1957, with Handwritten Note by Florida Governor LeRoy Collins, the World Digital Library. Last updated October 17, 2014. http://www.wdl. org/en/item/14196/.

Kahlenberg, Richard D. *Tough Liberal: Albert Shanker and the Battles Over Schools, Unions, Race, and Democracy.* New York: Columbia University Press, 2007.

Katz, Michael. *A History of Compulsory Education Laws, Fastback Series No 75.Bicentennial Series.* Bloomington, IN: Phi Delta Kappa, 1976.

Kennedy, President John F. *NASA – Excerpt from the 'Special Message to the Congress on Urgent National Needs'.*Delivered in-person before a joint session of Congress May 25, 1961.NASA website. Accessed January 2, 2016. https://www.nasa.gov/vision/space/features/jfk_speech_text.html#.VoSI5pMrJ8c.

Kern, Nora, and WentanaGebru. *Waiting Lists to Attend Charter Schools Top 1 Million Names,* National Alliance for Public Charter Schools, May 2014. http://www.publiccharters.org/wp-content/uploads/2014/05/NAPCS-2014-Wait-List-Report.pdf.

Khadaroo, Stacy Teicher. "How One Massachusetts Town Turned around Early Reading Program."*The Christian Science Monitor Online,* May 26, 2015. http://www.csmonitor.com/USA/Education/2015/0526/How-one-Massachusetts-town-turned-around-early-reading-program.

King, Martin Luther Jr. *Why We Can't Wait.* Boston, MA: Beacon Press, 1963.

Kirp, David L. T*he Wrong Kind of Education Reform: Three New Books Decimate the Case for Charter Schools and Vouchers.* Slate, September 4, 2013. http://www.slate.com/articles/news_and_politics/science/2013/09/charters_schools_and_vouchers_decimating_the_case_for_privatizing_public. html.

Kluger, Richard. *SimpleJustice: The History of Brown v. Board of Education and Black America's Struggle for Equality.* New York: Vintage Books, 1975.

Lamb, Elizabeth. *Pawloski Creates 'Culture of Success' for Impoverished Students.* SC Now Morning News Online. December 17, 2011. http://www.scnow.com/news/local/article_334df023-56c8-54fc-b302-a805c57eecba.html.

Layton, Lyndsey. "*California Court Rules Teacher Tenure Creates Impermissible Unequal Conditions."The Washington Post Online.* June 10, 2014. https://

www.washingtonpost.com/local/education/calif-court-rules-teacher-ten-ure-creates-unequal-conditions/2014/06/10/8be4f64a-f0be-11e3-914c-1fb-d0614e2d4_story.html.

Lindsay, CA Population: 2010 Census. Accessed January 24, 2016. http://census-viewer.com/city/CA/Lindsay.

The Lindsay Unified Strategic Design, Lindsay School District Online. Accessed January 27, 2016. http://www.lindsay.k12.ca.us/filelibrary/LUSD%20Strate-gic%20Design%201.pdf.

Logsdon, John M. *John F. Kennedy and the Race to the Moon*. New York: Palgrave Macmillan, 2010.

Luby, Joan, et al. "The Effects of Poverty on Childhood Brain Development: The Mediating Effect of Caregiving and Stressful Life Events." *JAMA Pediatrics* 167, no.12 (2013):1135–42. doi:10.1001/jamapediatrics.2013.3139. http://archpedi.jamanetwork.com/article.aspx?articleid=1761544.

Malden Public Schools Mission & Vision. Salemwood School. Accessed January 4, 2016. http://maldenps.org/salemwood/about/general-information/unique-featuresdescription-and-unique-features-description-and-unique-features-ms-keenan-principal-ckeenanmalden-mec-edu-k-4-office-781-3/.

Mathews, Jay. "Bush Pushes Vouchers, D.C. Charters." *The Washington Post Online*, July 2, 2003. https://www.washingtonpost.com/archive/politics/2003/07/02/bush-pushes-vouchers-dc-charters/3100af21-42f8-40d8-8641-1be2cd432a56/.

Mission. Village Leadership Academy. Accessed January 4, 2016. http://www.vlacademy.org/about-village-leadership-academy/missionvision/.

Mitra, Sugata. *Kids Can Teach Themselves*. LIFT 2007, TEDTalks filmed April 2007.Accessed January 2, 2016. https://www.ted.com/talks/sugata_mitra_shows_how_kids_teach_themselves.

Mitra, Sugata, and VivekRana. "Children and the Internet: Experiments with Minimally Invasive Education in India." *British Journal of Educational Technology* 32, no. 2 (2002): 221–32. http://hole-in-the-wall.com/docs/paper02.pdf.

Monastersky, Richard. *Researchers Gain Understanding of How Poverty Alters the Brain*. The Chronicle of Higher Education. February 18, 2008. http://chronicle.com/article/Researchers-Gain-Understand/516/.

Morton, Neal. "Judge May Rule Soon on Lawsuit Challenging Nevada Education Savings Accounts." *Las Vegas Review-Journal*, December 10, 2015. http://www.reviewjournal.com/news/education/judge-may-rule-soon-lawsuit-challeng-ing-nevada-education-savings-accounts.

Myers, Christine D. as cited by Christopher G. Bates. *The Early Republic and Antebellum America: An Encyclopedia of Social, Political, Cultural, and Economic History*. New York: Routledge, 2015.

"'Nation at Risk': The Best Thing or the Worst Thing for Education?" *USA Today Online*.updated August 1, 2008. http://usatoday30.usatoday.com/news/edu-cation/2008-04-22-nation-at-risk_N.htm.

A Nation at Risk: The Imperative for Educational Reform. National Commission on Excellence in Education. Last modified October 7, 1999. http://www2.ed.gov/pubs/NatAtRisk/index.html.

A Nation at Risk: Recommendations. US Department of Education, April 1983. https://www2.ed.gov/pubs/NatAtRisk/recomm.html.

New Orleans Public Schools Pre-Katrina and Now, by the Numbers.nola.com. August 29, 2014. http://www.nola.com/education/index.ssf/2014/08/new_ orleans_public_schools_pre.html.

Newport, Frank, and Joy Wilke. "Americans Rate Economy as Top Priority for Government." January 16, 2014.*Gallup Online*. http://www.gallup.com/ poll/166880/americans-rate-economy-top-priority-government.aspx.

Nobel Laureates by Age. The Official Website of the Novel Prize. Accessed January 4, 2016. http://www.nobelprize.org/nobel_prizes/lists/age.html.

Norton to Testify Against D.C. Voucher Bill at Rules Committee Today, Final Step Before Floor Vote Tomorrow, Congresswoman Eleanor Holmes Norton, October 20, 2015. https://norton.house.gov/media-center/press-releases/ norton-to-testify-against-dc-voucher-bill-at-rules-committee-today-final.

Number and Enrollment of Public Elementary and Secondary Schools, by School Level, Type, and Charter and Magnet Status: Selected Years, 1990–91 through 2012–13.*National Center for Education Statistics*. Accessed December 30, 2015. https://nces.ed.gov/programs/digest/d14/tables/dt14_216.20.asp. 149 Cong. Rec. 23,431 (2003).

Our Mission. Houston Heights Learning Academy Website. Accessed January 4, 2016. http://www.heightslearning.org/apps/pages/index.jsp?uREC_ ID=215004&type=d&pREC_ID=475320.

Overview and Inventory of State Requirements for School Coursework and Attendance. Research and Development Report, June 1992, National Center for Education Statistics. http://nces.ed.gov/pubs92/92663.pdf.

Paige, Rod, and Elaine Witty. *The Black-White Achievement Gap: Why Closing it Is the Civil Rights Issue of Our Time*. New York: AMACOM, 2010.

Paulson, Amanda. "*Education Reform: California to Join Race to the Top Rush.*"*The Christian Science Monitor Online*. January 5, 2010. http://www.csmonitor. com/USA/Education/2010/0105/Education-reform-California-to-join-Race-to-the-Top-rush.

Perlman, H., S. Usdin, and J. Button. "Using Popular Culture for Social Change: Soul City Videos and a Mobile Clip for Adolescents in South Africa." *Reproductive Health Matters*21, no. 41 (2013 May):31–34. doi: 10.1016/S0968-8080(13)41707-X. http://www.ncbi.nlm.nih.gov/pubmed/23684184.

PISA 2012 Results. The Organisation for Economic Co-operation and Development (OECD) Official Website. Accessed January 2, 2016. http://www.oecd. org/pisa/keyfindings/pisa-2012-results.htm.

Plessy v. Ferguson, 163 U.S. 537 (1896).

Policy Basics: Where Do Our State Tax Dollars Go? Center for Budget and Policy Priorities, April 14, 2015. http://www.cbpp.org/research/policy-basics-where-do-our-state-tax-dollars-go.

President Clinton and Charter Schools: A History Lesson. The Center for Education Reform, June 21, 2011. https://www.edreform.com/edspresso-shots/ president-clinton-and-charter-schools-a-history-lesson/.

Progress Is No Accident: Why ESEA Can't Backtrack on High School Graduation Rates. Alliance for Excellent Education. Accessed December 29, 2015. http:// all4ed.org/wp-content/uploads/2015/11/NoAccident.pdf.

Public School Expenditures. National Center for Education Statistics. Accessed January 2, 2016. http://nces.ed.gov/programs/coe/indicator_cmb.asp.

Quattrocchi, Christina. *How Lindsay Unified Redesigned Itself from The Ground Up, edSurge.* June 17, 2014. https://cedsurge.herokuapp.com/news/2014-06-17-how-lindsay-unified-redesigned-itself-from-the-ground-up.

Ravitch, Diane. "The Test of Time."*EducationNext Online,* Spring 2003, vol. 3, no. 2. http://educationnext.org/thetestoftime/.

Report: Public Schools More Segregated Now than 40 Years Ago. Washington Post Online, August 29, 2013. https://www.washingtonpost.com/news/answer-sheet/wp/2013/08/29/report-public-schools-more-segregated-now-than-40-years-ago/.

Rhee, Michelle. *My Break with the Democrats,* excerpted from Michelle Rhee's book "Radical: Fighting to Put Students First" and republished by The Daily Beast. February 4, 2013. http://www.thedailybeast.com/articles/2013/02/04/michelle-rhee-my-break-with-the-democrats.html.

Rich, Motoko. "As Graduation Rates Rise, Experts Fear Diplomas Come Up Short."*New York Times Online,* December 26, 2015. http://www.nytimes.com/2015/12/27/us/as-graduation-rates-rise-experts-fear-standards-have-fallen.html?_r=0.

Robert F. Kennedy: Remarks on the Assassination of Martin Luther King, Jr. American Rhetoric, Top 100 Speeches. Accessed December 29, 2015. http://www.americanrhetoric.com/speeches/rfkonmlkdeath.html.

Rogers, Abby. "'Will & Grace' Creator Explains How He Created A Successful Gay TV Show Using Ellen's Mistakes."*Business Insider,* February 5, 2013. http://www.businessinsider.com/max-mutchnick-explains-will-and-grace-2013-2.

Salemwood Elementary School, Public School Review Online. Accessed January 4, 2016. http://www.publicschoolreview.com/salemwood-elementary-school-profile. *School Choice Yearbook 2011-2012,* Alliance for School Choice. Accessed January 2, 2016. http://issuu.com/afc.yearbooks/docs/school_choice_yearbook_2011-12.

School Choice Info: What Is School Choice?. Parents for Choice in Education. Accessed December 30, 2015. http://www.choiceineducation.org/school-choice_faq.php.

*School Choice Yearbook 2012–2013.*Alliance for School Choice. Accessed January 2, 2016. http://issuu.com/afc.yearbooks/docs/school_choice_yearbook_2012-13.

School Choice Yearbook 2013–2014. Alliance for School Choice. Accessed January 2, 2016. http://issuu.com/afc.yearbooks/docs/afc_2013-14_yearbook.

School Desegregation and Equal Educational Opportunity. Leadership Conference on Civil Rights Education. Accessed December 29, 2015. http://www.civilrights.org/resources/civilrights101/desegregation.html.

Scott, Dylan. *48 percent of U.S. Schools Failed Federal Benchmarks.* Governing: The States and Localities, December 15, 2011. http://www.governing.com/news/local/gov-report-almost-half-US-schools-missed-AYP-2011.html.

"Segregation's Citadel Unbreached in 4 Years."*Washington Observer,* Sunday, May 11, 1958. Newspaper map. Geography and Map Division, Library of Congress Online. Accessed December 29, 2015. https://www.loc.gov/exhibits/brown/brown-aftermath.html.

Separate Is not Equal, Brown v. Board of Education: Five Communities since. Brown, Smithsonian National Museum of American History Online. Accessed

December 29, 2015. http://americanhistory.si.edu/brown/history/6-legacy/five-since-brown.html.

Shen, Yilan, and Alexander Berger, *Charter School Finance*. National Conference of State Legislatures, February 2011. http://www.ncsl.org/documents/educ/charterschoolfinance.pdf.

Simon, Stephanie. "States Weigh Turning Education Funds Over to Parents." *Politico Online*. February 6, 2015. http://www.politico.com/story/2015/02/state-education-savings-accounts-taxpayers-114966.

A Stagnant Nation: Why American Students Are Still at Risk. ED in '08, April 2008, The Eli and Edythe Broad Foundation. Accessed January 2, 2016. http://www.broadeducation.org/asset/1128-a%20stagnant%20nation.pdf.

State Education Reforms: State Support for School Choice and Other Options. National Center for Education Statistics. Accessed January 2, 2016. http://nces.ed.gov/programs/statereform/sss.asp.

Statement of Principles. Democrats for Education Reform. Accessed December 30, 2015. http://dfer.org/about-us/statement-of-principles/.

Stossel, John. "John Stossel's 'Stupid in America.'" *ABC News Online*. January 13, 2006. http://abcnews.go.com/2020/Stossel/story?id=1500338.

Thomas Jefferson: Creating a Virginia Republic. The Library of Congress Online. Accessed December 29, 2015. http://www.loc.gov/exhibits/jefferson/jeffrep.html.

Thomas Jefferson, *Notes on the State of Virginia*, 268, University of Virginia Library Online, accessed December 29, 2015, http://search.lib.virginia.edu/catalog/uva-lib:710304/view#openLayer/uva-lib:1195571/2486/1821/1/1/0.

2012 Accountability Data. Malden, Massachusetts Department of Elementary and Secondary Education. Accessed January 4, 2016. http://profiles.doe.mass.edu/accountability/report/district.aspx?orgtypecode=5&linkid=30&-fycode=2012&orgcode=01650000.

2014 Illinois School Report Cards: Village Leadership Academy. Chicago Tribune. Accessed January 4, 2016. http://schools.chicagotribune.com/school/village-leadership-academy_chicago.

Types of Educational Choice: School Vouchers. American Federation for Children. Accessed December 30, 2015. http://www.federationforchildren.org/ed-choice-101/types-educational-choice/.

United States: Key Findings, PISA Results from PISA 2012. OECD 2012. Accessed January 2, 2016. http://www.oecd.org/pisa/keyfindings/PISA-2012-results-US.pdf.

Vergara v. California, No. BC484642 (Cal. Super. Ct. Aug. 27, 2014), http://studentsmatter.org/wp-content/uploads/2014/08/SM_Final-Judgment_08.28.14.pdf. Decision has been appealed. Vergara v. California, No. B258589 (Cal. Ct. App.) (case pending).

Vietnamese Americans. Pew Research Center: Social & Demographic Trends. Accessed January 2, 2016. http://www.pewsocialtrends.org/asianamericans-graphics/vietnamese/.

Wallace in the Schoolhouse Door: Marking the 40th Anniversary of Alabama's Civil Rights Standoff, National Public Radio Online. Accessed December 29, 2015. http://www.npr.org/2003/06/11/1294680/wallace-in-the-schoolhouse-door.

Walls, David. *Environmental Movement.* Sonoma State University. Accessed January 2, 2016. http://www.sonoma.edu/users/w/wallsd/environmental-movement.shtml.

Welcome to ESA. Arizona Department of Education. Accessed January 2, 2016. http://www.azed.gov/esa/.

Wheelan, Charles. "Democrats Stand In The Schoolhouse Door On Vouchers." *The Philly.* June 1, 1999. http://articles.philly.com/1999-06-01/news/25497629_1_school-choice-vouchers-public-schools.

Wilgoren, Debbi, Valerie Strauss, and David A. Vise. "One Year Later, Becton Still Struggles." *the Washington Post Archives Online.* November 18, 1997. http://www.washingtonpost.com/wp-srv/local/longterm/library/dc/schools/becton2.htm.

"The Year of School Choice: No Fewer than 13 States Have Passed Major Education Reforms." *The Wall Street Journal Online.* July 5, 2011. http://www.wsj.com/articles/SB10001424052702304450604576420330972531442.

Yousafzai, Malala, and Christina Lamb. *I am Malala: The Girl Who Stood Up for Education and Was Shot by the Taliban.* London: Weidenfeld & Nicolson, 2013

Index